First World War
and Army of Occupation
War Diary
France, Belgium and Germany

48 DIVISION
Headquarters, Branches and Services
Commander Royal Engineers
29 March 1915 - 31 October 1917

WO95/2748/2

The Naval & Military Press Ltd
www.nmarchive.com
Published in association with The National Archives

Published by

The Naval & Military Press Ltd

Unit 10 Ridgewood Industrial Park,

Uckfield, East Sussex,

TN22 5QE England

Tel: +44 (0) 1825 749494

www.naval-military-press.com

www.nmarchive.com

This diary has been reprinted in facsimile from the original. Any imperfections are inevitably reproduced and the quality may fall short of modern type and cartographic standards.

© **Crown Copyright**
Images reproduced by permission of The National Archives, London, England, 2015.

Contents

Document type	Place/Title	Date From	Date To
Heading	WO95/2748 48 Div Com.R.E. Apr 15-Oct 17		
Heading	48th Division Bef C.R.E. Apr 1915 Oct 1917		
Heading	Hd Qrs. RE S.M. Division Vol I 29.3-30.4.15		
Heading	War Diary Of 1/1st South Midland Divisional Royal Engineers From 29th March 1915 To 30th April 1915		
War Diary	Braintree	29/03/1915	30/03/1915
War Diary	Chelmsford	30/03/1915	30/03/1915
War Diary	Le Havre	31/03/1915	30/04/1915
Heading	Hd. Qr R.E. 48th (SM) Division Vol II 1-31.5.15		
Heading	War Diary Of 48th (South Midland) Divisional Engineers From 1st May 1915 To 31st May 1915 (Volume 2)		
War Diary	Nieppe	01/05/1915	31/05/1915
Heading	48th Division Hd. Qrs. R.E. 48th Division Vol IIi 1-30.6.15		
Heading	War Diary Of 48th (South Midland) Divisional Engineers From 1st June 1915 To 30th June 1915 (Volume 3)		
War Diary	Nieppe	01/06/1915	27/06/1915
War Diary	Busnes	28/06/1915	30/06/1915
Heading	48th Division Hd Qrs R.E. 48th Division Vol IV 1-31-7-15		
Heading	War Diary Of 48th (South Midland) Divisional Engineers From 1st July 1915 To 31st July 1915 (Volume 4.)		
War Diary	Lillers	01/07/1915	10/07/1915
War Diary	Noeux Les Mines	11/07/1915	16/07/1915
War Diary	Lillers	17/07/1915	20/07/1915
War Diary	Authie	21/07/1915	31/07/1915
Heading	48th Division Hd Qrs R.E. 48th Division Vol V From 1-31.8.15		
Heading	War Diary Of 48th (South Midland) Divisional Engineers From 1st August 1915 To 31st August 1915 (Volume 5)		
War Diary	Authie	01/08/1915	03/08/1915
War Diary	Bus Les Artois	04/08/1915	31/08/1915
Heading	48th Division Hd Qrs R.E. 48th Division Vol VI Sept 15		
Heading	War Diary Of 48th (South Midland) Divisional Engineers From 1st September 1915 To 30th September 1915 (Volume 6)		
War Diary	Bus-Les-Artois	01/09/1915	30/09/1915
Heading	Hd. Qrs. R.E. 48th Division Vol VII Oct 15		
Heading	War Diary Of 48th (South Midland) Divisional Engineers From 1st October 1915 To 31st October 1915 (Volume 7)		
War Diary	Bus-Les-Artois	01/10/1915	31/10/1915
Heading	War Diary Of 48th (South Midland) Divisional Engineers From 1st November 1915 To 30th November 1915 (Volume 8)		

War Diary Heading	Bus-Les-Artois War Diary Of 48th (South Midland) Divisional Engineers From 1st December 1915 To 31st December 1915 (Volume 9)	01/11/1915	30/11/1915
War Diary Heading	Bus-Les-Artois War Diary Of 48th (South Midland) Divisional Engineers From 1st January 1916 To 31st January 1916 (Volume 10)	01/12/1915	31/12/1915
War Diary Heading	Bus-Les-Artois War Diary Of 48th (South Midland) Divisional Engineers From 1st February 1916 To 29th February 1916 Vol XI	01/01/1916	31/01/1916
War Diary Heading	Bus-Les-Artois War Diary Of 48th (South Midland) Divisional Engineers From 1st March 1916 To 31st March 1916	01/02/1916	29/02/1916
War Diary	Hem	18/05/1916	31/05/1916
War Diary Heading	Bus-Les-Artois War Diary Of 48th (South Midland) Divisional Engineers From 1st April 1916 To 30th April 1916 Vol XIII	01/03/1916	31/03/1916
War Diary Heading	Couin War Diary Of 48th (South Midland) Divisional Engineers From 1st May 1916 To 31st May 1916 (Volume 14)	01/04/1916	30/04/1916
War Diary Heading	Couin War Diary Of 48th (South Midland) Divisional Engineers From 1st June 1916 To 30th June 1916 (Volume 16)	01/05/1916	17/05/1916
War Diary Heading	Couin War Diary Of 48th (South Midland) Divisional Engineers From 1st July 1916 To 31st July 1916 (Volume 17)	01/06/1916	30/06/1916
War Diary	Couin	01/07/1916	27/07/1916
War Diary	Domqueur	28/07/1916	31/07/1916
Miscellaneous	Summary Of Engineer And Pioneer Work Carried Out By 48th Division In The Ovillers La Boisselle Area	27/07/1916	27/07/1916
Miscellaneous	Summary Of Engineer Work Executed During 24 Hours	27/07/1916	27/07/1916
Miscellaneous	48th Division Summary Of Engineers Work Executed During 24 Hours Ending 3-0 am 26-7-16	28/07/1916	28/07/1916
Miscellaneous	48th Division Summary Of Engineers Work Executed During 24 Hours Ending 3 am 26-7-16	26/07/1916	26/07/1916
Miscellaneous	48th Division Summary Of Engineers Work Executed During 24 Hours Ending 3 am 25-7-16	25/07/1916	25/07/1916
Miscellaneous	48th Division Summary Of Engineers Work Executed During 24 Hours Ending 3-0 am 24-7-16	24/07/1916	24/07/1916
Miscellaneous	48th Division Summary Of Engineers Work For 24 Hours Ending 3 a.m. 23.7.16	23/07/1916	23/07/1916
Miscellaneous	48th Division Summary Of Engineers Work For 24 Hours Ending 3 a.m. 22.7.16	22/07/1916	22/07/1916
Miscellaneous	Summary Of Engineer Work Carried Out During Night 20/21st	21/07/1916	21/07/1916
Miscellaneous	Summary Of Engineer Work Carried Out During 24 Hours	20/07/1916	20/07/1916
Miscellaneous	Summary Of Engineer Work Carried Out During 24 Hours	19/07/1916	19/07/1916

Miscellaneous	Summary Of R.E. Work Carried Out During Night	19/07/1916	19/07/1916
Miscellaneous	Summary Of Engineer Work Carried Out During 24 Hours	18/07/1916	18/07/1916
Heading	48th Divisional Engineers C.R.E. 48th Division August 1916		
War Diary	Domqueur	01/08/1916	08/08/1916
War Diary	Beauval	09/08/1916	12/08/1916
War Diary	Bouzincourt	13/08/1916	27/08/1916
War Diary	Bertrancourt	28/08/1916	31/08/1916
Miscellaneous	Report On Engineers Work Carried Out By The 48th Division	29/08/1916	29/08/1916
Heading	48th Divisional Engineers C.R.E. 48th Division September 1916		
Heading	War Diary Of 48th (South Midland) Divisional Engineers From 1st September 1916 To 30th September 1916 (Volume 19.)		
War Diary	Bertrancourt	01/09/1916	02/09/1916
War Diary	Beauval	03/09/1916	11/09/1916
War Diary	Hem	13/09/1916	18/09/1916
War Diary	Bernaville	24/09/1916	29/09/1916
War Diary	Henu	30/09/1916	30/09/1916
Heading	War Diary Of 48th (South Midland) Divisional Engineers From 1st October 1916 To 31st October 1916 (Volume 20)		
War Diary	Henu	01/10/1916	31/10/1916
Miscellaneous	48 Division Report On R.E. Work	04/10/1916	04/10/1916
Miscellaneous	48 Division Report On R.E. Work	05/10/1916	05/10/1916
Miscellaneous	48 Division Report On R.E. Work	06/10/1916	06/10/1916
Miscellaneous	48 Division Report On R.E. Work	07/10/1916	07/10/1916
Miscellaneous	Daily Work Report	09/10/1916	09/10/1916
Miscellaneous	Daily Work Report	08/10/1916	08/10/1916
Miscellaneous	Daily Work Report	10/10/1916	10/10/1916
Miscellaneous	Daily Work Report	11/10/1916	11/10/1916
Miscellaneous	Daily Work Report	12/10/1916	12/10/1916
Miscellaneous	Daily Work Report	13/10/1916	13/10/1916
Miscellaneous	Daily Work Report	14/10/1916	14/10/1916
Miscellaneous	Daily Work Report	15/10/1916	15/10/1916
Miscellaneous	Daily Work Report	16/10/1916	16/10/1916
Miscellaneous	Daily Work Report	17/10/1916	17/10/1916
Miscellaneous	Daily Work Report	18/10/1916	18/10/1916
Miscellaneous	Daily Work Report	19/10/1916	19/10/1916
Heading	War Diary Of 48th (South Midland) Divisional Engineers From 1st November 1916 To 30th November 1916 (Volume 21)		
Miscellaneous	Daily Work Report	20/10/1916	20/10/1916
War Diary	Millencourt	01/11/1916	30/11/1916
Miscellaneous	48th Division Progress Report for 24 Hours Ending Noon 30-11-16	30/11/1916	30/11/1916
Miscellaneous	48th Division Progress Report for 24 Hours Ending Noon 29-11-16	29/11/1916	29/11/1916
Miscellaneous	48th Division Progress Report for 24 Hours Ending Noon 28-11-16	28/11/1916	28/11/1916
Miscellaneous	48th Division Progress Report for 24 Hours Ending Noon 27-11-16	27/11/1916	27/11/1916
Miscellaneous	48th Division Progress Report for 24 Hours Ending Noon 26-11-16	26/11/1916	26/11/1916

Miscellaneous	48th Division Progress Report for 24 Hours Ending Noon 25-11-16	25/11/1916	25/11/1916
Miscellaneous	48th Division Progress Report for 24 Hours Ending Noon 24-11-16	24/11/1916	24/11/1916
Miscellaneous	48th Division Progress Report for 24 Hours Ending Noon 23-11-16	23/11/1916	23/11/1916
Miscellaneous	48th Division Progress Report for 24 Hours Ending Noon 22-11-16	22/11/1916	22/11/1916
Miscellaneous	48th Division Progress Report for 24 Hours Ending Noon 21-11-16	21/11/1916	21/11/1916
Miscellaneous	48th Division Progress Report for 24 Hours Ending Noon 20-11-16	20/11/1916	20/11/1916
Miscellaneous	48th Division Progress Report for 24 Hours Ending Noon 19-11-16	19/11/1916	19/11/1916
Miscellaneous	48th Division Progress Report for 24 Hours Ending Noon 18-11-16	18/11/1916	18/11/1916
Miscellaneous	48th Division Progress Report for 24 Hours Ending Noon 17-11-16	17/11/1916	17/11/1916
Miscellaneous	48th Division Progress Report for 24 Hours Ending Noon 16-11-16	16/11/1916	16/11/1916
Miscellaneous	48th Division Progress Report for 24 Hours Ending Noon 15-11-16	15/11/1916	15/11/1916
Miscellaneous	48th Division Progress Report for 24 Hours Ending Noon 14-11-16	14/11/1916	14/11/1916
Miscellaneous	48th Division Progress Report for 24 Hours Ending Noon 13-11-16	13/11/1916	13/11/1916
Miscellaneous	48th Division Progress Report for 24 Hours Ending Noon 12-11-16	12/11/1916	12/11/1916
Miscellaneous	48th Division Progress Report for 24 Hours Ending Noon 11-11-16	11/11/1916	11/11/1916
Miscellaneous	48th Division Progress Report for 24 Hours Ending Noon 10-11-16	10/11/1916	10/11/1916
Miscellaneous	48th Division Progress Report for 24 Hours Ending Noon 9-11-16	09/11/1916	09/11/1916
Miscellaneous	48th Division Progress Report for 24 Hours Ending Noon 8-11-16	08/11/1916	08/11/1916
Miscellaneous	48th Division Progress Report for 24 Hours Ending Noon 7-11-16	07/11/1916	07/11/1916
Miscellaneous	48th Division Progress Report for 24 Hours Ending Noon 6-11-16	06/11/1916	06/11/1916
Miscellaneous	48th Division Progress Report for 24 Hours Ending Noon 5-11-16	05/11/1916	05/11/1916
Miscellaneous	48th Division Progress Report for 24 Hours Ending Noon 4-11-16	04/11/1916	04/11/1916
Miscellaneous	48th Division Progress Report for 24 Hours Ending Noon 3-11-16	03/11/1916	03/11/1916
Heading	War Diary Of 48th (South Midland) Divisional Engineers From 1st December 1916 To 31st December 1916 (Volume 22)		
War Diary	Lozenge Wood Fricourt	01/12/1916	16/12/1916
War Diary	Albert	16/12/1916	31/12/1916
Miscellaneous	48th Division Progress Report for 24 Hours Ending Noon 15-12-16	15/12/1916	15/12/1916
Miscellaneous	48th Division Progress Report for 24 Hours Ending Noon 14-12-16	14/12/1916	14/12/1916

Miscellaneous	48th Division Progress Report for 24 Hours Ending Noon 13-12-16	13/12/1916	13/12/1916
Miscellaneous	48th Division Progress Report for 24 Hours Ending Noon 12-12-16	12/12/1916	12/12/1916
Miscellaneous	48th Division Progress Report for 24 Hours Ending Noon 11-12-16	11/12/1916	11/12/1916
Miscellaneous	48th Division Progress Report for 24 Hours Ending Noon 10-12-16	10/12/1916	10/12/1916
Miscellaneous	48th Division Progress Report for 24 Hours Ending Noon 9-12-16	09/12/1916	09/12/1916
Miscellaneous	48th Division Progress Report for 24 Hours Ending Noon 8-12-16	08/12/1916	08/12/1916
Miscellaneous	48th Division Progress Report for 24 Hours Ending Noon 7-12-16	07/12/1916	07/12/1916
Miscellaneous	48th Division Progress Report for 24 Hours Ending Noon 6-12-16	06/12/1916	06/12/1916
Miscellaneous	48th Division Progress Report for 24 Hours Ending Noon 5-12-16	05/12/1916	05/12/1916
Miscellaneous	48th Division Progress Report for 24 Hours Ending Noon 4-12-16	04/12/1916	04/12/1916
Miscellaneous	48th Division Progress Report for 24 Hours Ending Noon 3-12-16	03/12/1916	03/12/1916
Miscellaneous	48th Division Progress Report for 24 Hours Ending Noon 2-12-16	02/12/1916	02/12/1916
Miscellaneous	48th Division Progress Report for 24 Hours Ending Noon 1-12-16	01/12/1916	01/12/1916
Map	Map		
Map	Buried Cable Routes		
Miscellaneous			
Heading	War Diary Of 48th (South Midland) Divisional Engineers From 1st January 1917 To 31st January 1917 (Volume 23)		
War Diary	Albert	01/01/1917	02/01/1917
War Diary	Baizieux	03/01/1917	25/01/1917
War Diary	Cappy	26/01/1917	31/01/1917
Heading	War Diary Of 48th (South Midland) Divisional Engineers From 1st February 1917 To 28th February 1917 (Volume 24)		
War Diary	Cappy	01/02/1917	28/02/1917
Heading	War Diary Of 48th (South Midland) Divisional Engineers From 1st March 1917 To 31st March 1917 (Volume 25)		
War Diary	Cappy	01/03/1917	24/03/1917
War Diary	Peronne	25/03/1917	31/03/1917
Heading	War Diary Of 48th (South Midland) Divisional Engineers From 1st April 1917 To 30th April 1917 (Volume 25)		
War Diary	Peronne	01/04/1917	01/04/1917
War Diary	Tincourt	02/04/1917	22/04/1917
War Diary	K.11.a.79	23/04/1917	29/04/1917
Heading	War Diary Of 48th (South Midland) Divisional Engineers From 1st May 1917 To 31st May 1917 (Volume 26)		
War Diary	K.11.a.79	01/05/1917	15/05/1917
War Diary	Beaulencourt	16/05/1917	24/05/1917
War Diary	Haplincourt	25/05/1917	31/05/1917

Heading	War Diary Of 48th (South Midland) Divisional Engineers From 1st June 1917 To 30th June 1917 (Volume 27)		
War Diary	Haplincourt (I 34 A 25)	01/06/1917	30/06/1917
Heading	War Diary Of 48th (South Midland) Divisional Engineers From 1st July 1917 To 31st July 1917 (Volume 28)		
War Diary	Haplincourt (I 34a25)	01/07/1917	04/07/1917
War Diary	Gomiecourt	05/07/1917	31/07/1917
Heading	War Diary Of 48th (South Midland) Divisional Engineers From 1st August 1917 To 31st August 1917 (Volume 29)		
War Diary	Border Camp Nr. Poperinghe	01/08/1917	26/08/1917
War Diary	Canal Bank Nr. Ypres	27/08/1917	31/08/1917
Heading	War Diary Of 48th (South Midland) Divisional Engineers From 1st September 1917 To 30th September 1917 (Volume 30)		
War Diary	Poperinghe-Elverdinghe Road A.23.c.14	01/09/1917	28/09/1917
War Diary	Brake Camp	29/09/1917	30/09/1917
Heading	War Diary Of 48th (South Midland) Divisional Engineers From 1st October 1917 To 31st October 1917 (Volume 31)		
War Diary	Brake Camp G.6.b.19	01/10/1917	09/10/1917
War Diary	Canal Bank C.25.d.15	04/10/1917	14/10/1917
War Diary	La Targette	15/10/1917	31/10/1917

WO95/2748
48 Div
Com. R.E
Apr '15 - Oct '17

48TH DIVISION

BEF

C. R. E.
APR 1915-MAR 1919

Oct 1917

To ITALY

131/5140

Hd. Qu. RE. (48) S.M. Division.

Vol I. 27.3 — 30.4.15

Mar 15

CONFIDENTIAL.
****

WAR DIARY.

of

1/1st South Midland Divisional Royal Engineers.

From 29th March 1915.................to......................30th April 1915.

(Volume   )

Army Form C. 2118.

WAR DIARY
or
INTELLIGENCE SUMMARY.
(Erase heading not required.)

Instructions regarding War Diaries and Intelligence Summaries are contained in F. S. Regs., Part II. and the Staff Manual respectively. Title pages will be prepared in manuscript.

Place	Date 1915.	Hour	Summary of Events and Information	Remarks and references to Appendices
	March			
BRAINTREE	29		2nd Field Company left BRAINTREE in two parts and marched to CHELMSFORD where they entrained that night.	
BRAINTREE.	29.		Headquarters less C.R.E. and Adjutant and M.O. went to SPRINGFIELD in the afternoon.	
do.	30.		C.R.E., Adjutant and M.O. went by car from BRAINTREE to CHELMSFORD arriving there at 10 a.m. Met the remainder of Headquarters at the station.	
CHELMSFORD.			Headquarters entrained for SOUTHAMPTON with Divisional Cyclists Company and arrived at SOUTHAMPTON about 5 p.m. Embarked on s.s. City of Dunkirk - C.R.E. senior officer on board, O.C. Troops.	
LE HAVRE.	31.		Arrived at LE HAVRE 10 a.m. Met 2nd Field Company who landed shortly after. Remained at LE HAVRE that day and night. M. Sichel-Dulong reported himself as Interpreter attached to Headquarters.	

Army Form C. 2118.

WAR DIARY
or
INTELLIGENCE SUMMARY.

(Erase heading not required.)

Instructions regarding War Diaries and Intelligence Summaries are contained in F. S. Regs., Part II. and the Staff Manual respectively. Title pages will be prepared in manuscript.

Place	Date 1915.	Hour	Summary of Events and Information	Remarks and references to Appendices
Le Havre.	April. 1.	10.30 a.m.	Headquarters and 2nd Field Company entrained at 6 a.m. and left LE HAVRE Goods Station 10.30 a.m.	
	2.		Arrived at BAVINCHOVE Station (Cassell) about 6 a.m., marched to LESTROIS ROIS and billeted. Horses picketed in field. C.R.E. reported arrival at Divisional Headquarters at OXELAERE.	
	3.		Remained at LES TROIS ROIS.	
	4.		Remained at LES TROIS ROIS. Col. Simpson-Baikie called with Capt. Girdwood and explained the move for the following day. Arranged to have route reconnoitered.	
	5.		R.E. Headquarters and 2nd Field Company left LES TROIS ROIS at 10 a.m. and marched to FLETRE, via STAPLE and CAESTRE. Thence to farm LE COQ DE PAILLE and went into billets.	Heavy rain.
	6.		Remained at LE COQ DE PAILLE. Capt. Livesay and Major Law called and gave instructions regarding attachment to 4th Division.	
	7.		Capt. Hosegood and the 1/1st Field Company marched over from MERRIS. The 1/2nd Field Company left LE COQ DE PAILLE at 1 p.m. to join S.M. Infantry Brigade and marched to PLOEGSTEERT via NIEPPE. C.R.E. and Adjutant left by car at 2.30 p.m. for NIEPPE and reported to C.R.E., 4th Divn. Headquarters, lead C.R.E. and Adjutant, went with 1/1st Field Company to farm near MERRIS.	
	8.		C.R.E. and Adjutant attached 4th Division. Visited the trenches at LE TOUQUET with Major Symons, O.C., 7th Field Company, R.E.	
	9.		Went with Major Hoysted, O.C., 9th Field Co., R.E., to second line through PLOEGSTEERT WOOD.	

Army Form C. 2118.

WAR DIARY
or
INTELLIGENCE SUMMARY.

(Erase heading not required.)

Instructions regarding War Diaries and Intelligence Summaries are contained in F. S. Regs., Part II. and the Staff Manual respectively. Title pages will be prepared in manuscript.

Place	Date 1915.	Hour	Summary of Events and Information	Remarks and references to Appendices
	April. 10.	Night.	Went with C.R.E., 4th Division and Major Hoysted to the trenches in front of PLOEGSTEERT WOOD and at ST. YVES.	
	11.		C.R.E. and Adjutant went to destroyed villa on HILL 63, part of which was being blown down by 2nd Field Company to obtain bricks.	
	12.		Left NIEPPE by motor car in afternoon and arrived at OUTTERSTEENE where the remainder of the R.E. Divisional Headquarters joined.	
	13.		At OUTTERSTEENE. C.R.E. called on General Glubb, C.E., 3rd Corps.	
	14.		At OUTTERSTEENE. Adjutant visited R.E. Park at STRAZEELE.	
	15.		At OUTTERSTEENE. C.R.E. and Adjutant went by car to NIEPPE and on to ROMARIN and selected site for R.E. Store.	
	16.		R.E. Headquarters marched to NIEPPE and billeted.	
	17.	Night.	NIEPPE. C.R.E. and Adjutant went with Major Hoysted and Capt. Livesay to the left trenches of the Warwickshire Brigade.	
	18.	Night.	C.R.E. instructed to report to R.E. Office at ROUEN. C.R.E. and Adjutant went with Lt. Col. Simpson-Baikie and Major Hoysted to portion of trenches occupied by S.M. Brigade and Glos. and Worc. Brigade. Half 9th Field Company R.E. and West Lancs Field Co., R.E. joined.	
	19.		Lt. Col. E. S. Sinnott left. Lt. Col. H.J.M. Marshall joined as C.R.E. C.R.E. and Adjutant inspected communication trenches at STINKING FARM and LE ROSIGNOLS.	
	20.	Night.	C.R.E. and Adjutant visited trenches near PROWSE POINT.	

Army Form C. 2118.

WAR DIARY
or
INTELLIGENCE SUMMARY.

(Erase heading not required.)

Instructions regarding War Diaries and Intelligence Summaries are contained in F.S. Regs., Part II. and the Staff Manual respectively. Title pages will be prepared in manuscript.

Place	Date 1915-	Hour	Summary of Events and Information	Remarks and references to Appendices
	April. 21.	Night.	Adjutant saw G.O.C., Glos. & Worc. Brigade re question of stores. C.R.E. and Adjutant visited trenches near STINKING FARM and LE ROSIGNOL.	Weather dry and fine throughout the month, especially latter half.
	22.		Adjutant visited timber yard at ARMENTIERES. Decision received re junction with North Midland Division.	
	23.		C.R.E. and Adjutant visited ST. QUENTIN; Decision arrived at re Defence Line.	
	24.		C.R.E. attended conference 3rd Corps at BAILLEUL re 4th Pivot.	
	25.		Met General Feetham, G.O.C., North Staff. Brigade at ST. QUENTIN; visited LA PLUS DOUCE.	
	26.		C.R.E. and Adjutant visited LE ROSIGNOL and 2nd Pivot.	
	27.	Night.	C.R.E. and Adjutant visited DOUVE section and 2nd Pivot with O.C. 7th Field Co., R.E.	
	28.	Night.	C.R.E. and Adjutant visited ST. YVES and Mines Section. 7th Field Co., R.E. joined. Half 9th Field Co. R.E. and West Lancs Field Co. R.E. left.	
	29.		C.R.E. saw C.R.E. 4th Division in connection with certain works. Lieut. M. Whitwill, 1/2nd Field Company was shot through the arm on the night 29/30 April 1915.	
	30.		C.R.E. and Adjutant visited trenches on right of line.	

Major. R.E.
for C.R.E. S.M.D.

12/154/82

H.d. Qrs R.E. 48th (JM) Division

Vol II 1—31.5.15

CONFIDENTIAL.
****

W A R   DIARY.

of

48th (South Midland) Divisional Engineers.

From 1st May 1915..................to..........................31st May 1915.

(Volume 2.)

WAR DIARY

INTELLIGENCE SUMMARY.

(Erase heading not required.)

Army Form C. 2118.

Instructions regarding War Diaries and Intelligence Summaries are contained in F.S. Regs., Part II. and the Staff Manual respectively. Title pages will be prepared in manuscript.

Place	Date 1915.	Hour	Summary of Events and Information	Remarks and references to Appendices
NIEPPE.	May. 1.		C.R.E. and Adjutant went with C.E. to 4th and 2nd Pivots and LA PLUS DOUCE. 1st S.M. Field Company joined.	
	2.		Bishop of Pretoria took Divine Service.	
	3.		C.R.E. and C.E. visited HILL 63.	
	4.		C.R.E. and Adjutant visited site of new works in PLOEGSTEERT.	
	5.		C.R.E. visited trenches with G.O.C. S.M. Brigade. C.E. visited office and Adjutant visited ARMENTIERES, BAILLEUL and STRAZEELE.	
	6.		C.R.E. accompanied G.O.C., S.M.D. to HILL 63. Adjutant went with D.A.A. & Q.M.G. and Sanitary Officer to inspect new site for Headquarters.	
	7.		C.R.E. went to see C.R.E., 6th Division and O.C. 174th Company in reference to Gas "Retort" experiments.	
	8.		C.R.E. went with C.E. to PLOEGSTEERT new works and on to store at ROMARIN to see various samples of trench appliances.	
	9.		C.R.E. visited works at PLOEGSTEERT WOOD.	
	10.		C.R.E. and Adjutant visited site for new works on HILL 63 and reconnoitered ground for a by pass road to HYDE PARK CORNER.	
	11.		C.R.E. and Q. visited proposed new site for Headquarters. C.R.E. and A.D.M.S. visited HILL 63 in regard to dug-outs. Adjutant visited Warwick Brigade Headquarters.	

Army Form C. 2118.

WAR DIARY
or
INTELLIGENCE SUMMARY.
(Erase heading not required.)

Instructions regarding War Diaries and Intelligence Summaries are contained in F. S. Regs., Part II. and the Staff Manual respectively. Title pages will be prepared in manuscript.

Place	Date 1915.	Hour	Summary of Events and Information	Remarks and references to Appendices
NIEPPE.	May 12.		C.E. and C.R.E. visited front line at PROWSE POINT and new works in PLOEGSTEERT. C.R.E. and Adjutant visited LA CRECHE. 1/2nd Field Company Headquarters moved from PLOEGSTEERT.	
	13.		C.R.E. and Adjutant visited LA CRECHE. C.R.E. instructed representatives of Battalions regarding manufacture and handling of Bombs. They were also shown sample arrangements for improvement of observation and fire from trenches. C.R.E. visited 4th Pivot. Adjutant and D.A.Q. visited OOSTHOVE FARM regarding new billets for 7th Field Co.	Rained all day.
	14.		C.R.E. visited HILL 63. 7th Field Company moved from PLOEGSTEERT.	Showery.
	15.		C.R.E. visited trenches near GERMAN HOUSE. Adjutant saw G.O.C. 144th Brigade and Staff Captain 145th Brigade re material for front line.	
	16.		C.R.E. and Adjutant accompanied C.E. to HILL 63.	Poured with rain
	17.		C.R.E. visited new works or HILL 63. Adjutant visited LA CRECHE.	
	18.		C.R.E. visited 1st Field Company and PLOEGSTEERT. C.R.E. and Adjutant visited LA CRECHE camp works.	Wet.
	19.		C.R.E. and Adjutant visited HILL 63, new works in PLOEGSTEERT, timber yard and Basseaut shops in Armentieres.	

- 3 -

Army Form C. 2118.

WAR DIARY

INTELLIGENCE SUMMARY

(Erase heading not required.)

Instructions regarding War Diaries and Intelligence Summaries are contained in F. S. Regs., Part II. and the Staff Manual respectively. Title pages will be prepared in manuscript.

Place	Date 1915.	Hour	Summary of Events and Information	Remarks and references to Appendices
NIEPPE.	May. 20.		C.R.E. visited LE ROSSIGNOL. Adjutant visited BAILLEUL.	Weather:- Fine and hot.
	21.		Routine.	
	22.		C.R.E. and C.E. visited Subsidiary line near HILL 63. Adjutant visited JONESVILLE.	
	23.		C.R.E. and Adjutant visited LA CRECHE and JONESVILLE.	
	24.		C.R.E. and Adjutant visited left portion of front line.	
	25.		C.R.E. visited point above LA PLUS DOUCE with C.E's 2nd and 3rd Corps. C.R.E. visited right of subsidiary line with C.E.	
	26.		C.R.E. and Adjutant visited LA CRECHE.	
	27.		C.R.E. visited HILL 63.	
	28.	Night.	C.R.E. visited certain sites with O.C., R.G.A. C.R.E. and Adjutant selected supporting points on left of line and visited left of front line.	
	29.		C.R.E. and Adjutant visited supporting points on right of line. C.E. called and explained to Adjutant what he required done in the matter of certain supporting points.	
	30.		C.R.E. visited HILL 63. Adjutant visited PLOEGSTEERT WOOD and trench 32.	
	31.		Routine.	

O. Frandon.
Major, R.E.
for C.R.E. S.M.D.

121/5885

48th Division

HdQrs R.E. 48th Division.

Vol III 1 — 30.6.15.

CONFIDENTIAL.
****

WAR DIARY

of

48th (South Midland) Divisional Engineers.

From 1st June 1915...............to...............30th June 1915.

(Volume 3)

Army Form C. 2118.

WAR DIARY
or
INTELLIGENCE SUMMARY.
(Erase heading not required.)

Instructions regarding War Diaries and Intelligence Summaries are contained in F. S. Regs., Part II. and the Staff Manual respectively. Title pages will be prepared in manuscript.

Place	Date 1915.	Hour	Summary of Events and Information	Remarks and references to Appendices
NIEPPE.	June 1.		C.R.E. accompanied Corps Commander to HILL 63. Adjutant visited BAILLEUL.	
	2.		C.R.E. selected sites for work in PLOEGSTEERT WOOD. Adjutant visited JONESVILLE re water supply.	
	3.		C.R.E. selected sites for new huts. Adjutant met G.O.C., 3rd Corps and C.E. at R.E. Store, ROMARIN; they also visited 1st and 2nd S.M. Field Co's workshops.	
	4.		C.R.E. visited ground near ST. YVES. C.E. visited left of front line Adjutant visited BAILLEUL and ARMENTIERES.	
	5.		C.R.E. visited hut sites on HILL 63. C.R.E. and Adjutant visited Trench 32. Blew up two mines in the German trenches in the BIRDCAGE.	
	6.		C.R.E. and Adjutant visited front line near CONVENT.	Hot and fine.
	7.		C.R.E. and Adjutant visited works on HILL 63 and selected sites for Headquarter Observation posts and for G.O.C's report centre and dug-outs. Enemy exploded mine in front of HAMPSHIRE T. without damaging our parapet or wire.	
	8.		G.O.C. inspected Lt. Cloutman and detachment of 174th Co., R.E. and congratulated them on their work in connection with the mine. C.R.E. visited HAMPSHIRE trench and viewed German mine.	
	9.		C.R.E. visited KRAAKENBERG and hutting on HILL 63. Adjutant selected billets with D.A.Q.M.G. for 2/1st S. M. Field Co. 2/1st S.M. Field Co. arrived.	Very heavy rain at night.
	10.		C.R.E. visited HILL 63, communication trenches by ASH HOUSE and PLOEGSTEERT WOOD.	

Army Form C. 2118.

WAR DIARY

INTELLIGENCE SUMMARY.

(Erase heading not required.)

Instructions regarding War Diaries and Intelligence Summaries are contained in F. S. Regs., Part II. and the Staff Manual respectively. Title pages will be prepared in manuscript.

Place	Date 1915.	Hour	Summary of Events and Information	Remarks and references to Appendices
NIEPPE.	June. 11.		Adjutant visited ARMENTIERES and BAILLEUL.	
	12.		C.R.E. visited PLOEGSTEERT WOOD. Adjutant visited ARMENTIERES.	
	13.		C.R.E. visited Hill 63. Adjutant visited Trench 31 and PLOEGSTEERT WOOD.	
	14.		Adjutant visited ARMENTIERES. Enemy exploded mine at 2.30 a.m. without damaging our parapet or wire, in front of trench 31.	
	15.		C.R.E. visited PLOEGSTEERT WOOD. Adjutant selected landing site for brushwood on Canal and visited BAILLEUL.	
	16.	Night. Day.	Adjutant visited Brigade Headquarters on the right regarding a mine; listening. R.E. Store closed at ROMARIN.	
	16.		C.R.E. and Adjutant visited new huts and works west of 63. Adjutant reconnoitered new approach road for reinforcements., and visited timber yard Armentieres. R.E. store re-opened at NIEPPE.	Very fine.
	17.		C.R.E. visited HILL 63 (and Stinking Farm.)	
	18.		C.R.E. visited HILL 63, huts and attended G.O.C's conference. Adjutant visited huts on 63 and timber yard at ARMENTIERES.	
	19.		C.R.E. visited HILL 63 and left section front trenches with C.E. Adjutant visited huts.	
	20.		C.R.E. visited line north of DOUVE. Adjutant reconnoitered a farm required for certain experiments with C.R.E., 3rd Corps.	
	21.		Adjutant visited farm selected for experiments, and huts.	

Army Form C. 2118.

WAR DIARY
INTELLIGENCE SUMMARY.
(Erase heading not required.)

- 3 -

Instructions regarding War Diaries and Intelligence Summaries are contained in F. S. Regs., Part II. and the Staff Manual respectively. Title pages will be prepared in manuscript.

Place	Date 1915.	Hour	Summary of Events and Information	Remarks and references to Appendices
NIEPPE.	June 22.		C.R.E. visited communication trench north of DOUVE and front line trench on left. Adjutant visited STEENWERCK, LA CRECHE and ARMENTIERES.	
	23.		Adjutant visited works at Chateau.	
	24.		C.R.E. attended conference at C.R.E's office. Adjutant visited works at Chateau. Arrangements being made for handing over to relieving Division. 1/1st Field Company, R.E. handed over to R.E. Company of 12th Division and marched out.	
	25.		Made arrangements for handing over with C.R.Es. 12th and Canadian Divisions. 1/2nd Field Company, R.E. handed over to R.E. Company of 12th Division and marched out.	
	26.		C.R.E. accompanied C.R.Es. 12th and Canadian Divisions round the trench line. Adjutant handed over stores etc. to representatives of Divisions. 2/1st Field Company, R.E. handed over to R.E. Company of Canadian Division and marched out.	
	27.		Headquarters R.E. marched at 5.30 a.m. with Divisional Headquarters Column to VIEUX BERQUIN and arrived there at 10 a.m. Marched again at 7.20 p.m. to BUSNES, via MERVILLE; arrived there about 12 midnight.	Cool, sunless day. Heavy rain at Vieux Berquin.
BUSNES.	28.		At Busnes.	
	29.		At Busnes.	
	30.		Headquarters, R.E. moved to LILLERS.	

[signature] Major R.E.
for C.R.E. 46th Div.

48th Division

101/6250

H.Q. R.E. 48th Division

Vol IV

1-31-7-15

CONFIDENTIAL.
****

WAR DIARY

of

48th (South Midland) Divisional Engineers.

From 1st July 1915................................31st July 1915.

(Volume 4.)

Army Form C. 2118.

WAR DIARY
or
INTELLIGENCE SUMMARY.
(Erase heading not required.)

Instructions regarding War Diaries and Intelligence Summaries are contained in F. S. Regs., Part II. and the Staff Manual respectively. Title pages will be prepared in manuscript.

Place	Date 1915.	Hour	Summary of Events and Information	Remarks and references to Appendices
LILLERS.	July 1.		Routine.	
	2.		Routine.	Very hot.
	3.		C.R.E. visited C.R.E., 47th Division.	
	4.		C.R.E. and Adjutant visited left sector of front line with representative of 47th Div. 3rd Field Company moved to LABOURSE for attachment to 1st Division.	
	5.		C.R.E. and Adjutant visited right sector of front line with representative of 47th Div.	
	6.		Routine.	
	7.		C.R.E. attended tactical exercises.	
	8.		C.R.E. visited C.R.E. 1st Division. Adjutant attended tactical exercises.	
	9.		Adjutant visited BETHUNE.	
	10.		C.R.E. visited C.E. Adjutant visited BAILLEUL, NIEPPE and ST. VENANT.	
NOEUX LES MINES.	11.		Hd. Qrs. R.E. moved to NOEUX LES MINES. 1st Field Company moved to near BRUAY. 2nd Field Company moved to near LABOURSE for attachment to 1st Division.	
	12.		1st and 2nd Field Companies moved forward with a view to taking over front line from 47th Division and 3rd Field Company moved to NOEUX LES MINES. After completion of moves orders were cancelled and 1st and 2nd Companies moved back to LABOURSE same night.	
	13.		Orders received to carry on with 2nd Line work as before moves of 12th inst. 1st Field Company moved back to near BRUAY. 3rd Field Company moved back to near LABOURSE.	

Army Form C. 2118.

WAR DIARY
or
INTELLIGENCE SUMMARY.
(Erase heading not required.)

Instructions regarding War Diaries and Intelligence Summaries are contained in F. S. Regs., Part II. and the Staff Manual respectively. Title pages will be prepared in manuscript.

Place	1915 Date	Hour	Summary of Events and Information	Remarks and references to Appendices
NEOUX LES MINES.	July 14.		C.R.E. and Adjutant visited work on second line.	
	15.		C.R.E. and Adjutant visited 2nd Line. Capt. A.J.M. Wright, 2nd S.M. Field Company acted as Adjutant during absence on leave of Major O. G. Brandon, R.E. (15th – 22nd).	
	16.		Headquarters R.E. moved back to LILLERS. 2nd S.M. Field Co. moved back to CAUCHY-A-LA-TOUR. 3rd S.M. Field Co. moved to RAIMBERT.	
LILLERS.	17.		At LILLERS. 1st S.M. Field Company moved to BELLERY.	
	18.		C.R.E. proceeded to TERRAMESNIL, and visited left sector of trenches and HEBUTERNE defences and French R.E. Park with French C.R.E.	
	19.		Headquarters R.E. and 1st S.M. Field Company entrained at BERGUETTE and arrived at DOULLENS at 10.30 a.m. Hd. Qrs. marches to TERRAMESNIL and 1st Field Co. to SARTON. 2nd S.M. Field Co. entrained at BERGUETTE, arrived at DOULLENS 1 p.m. and marched to BEAUQUESNE. 3rd S.M. Field Co. entrained at BERGUETTE and marched from DOULLENS to AUTHIE.	
	20.		Hd. Qrs. R.E. moved to AUTHIE and.	
AUTHIE.	21.		1st S.M. Field Co. moved to COIGNEUX, less Pontoon Section who moved to AUTHIE. 2nd S.M.Field Co. Headquarters Section and tool carts moved to AUTHIE and remainder of Company marched to COURCELLES. One section of 3rd Field Company proceeded to MARIEUX for work under 7th Corps.	
	22.		C.R.E. visited HEBUTERNE.	
	23.		C.R.E. and Capt. Wright visited front line right sector.	

Army Form C. 2118.

- 3 -

WAR DIARY
or
INTELLIGENCE SUMMARY.
(Erase heading not required.)

Instructions regarding War Diaries and Intelligence Summaries are contained in F. S. Regs., Part II. and the Staff Manual respectively. Title pages will be prepared in manuscript.

Place	Date 1915.	Hour	Summary of Events and Information	Remarks and references to Appendices
AUTHIE.	July. 24.		C.R.E. visited Second Line. 1st S.M. Field Company moved to HEBUTERNE less one section who moved to SAILLY-AU-BOIS. N.C.O. and 7 men of 3rd Field Company reported at BEAUQUESNE for work at 3rd Army Hd. Qrs.	
	25.		C.R.E. visited HEBUTERNE defences. Two sections of 2nd Field Company moved to BOIS DU WARNIMONT.	
	26.		C.R.E. reconnoitered site for Baths etc. with S.S.O. and location of supporting point east of BAYENCOURT. Adjutant visited DOULLENS; made arrangements for R.E. Park at SAILLY-AU-BOIS and reconnoitered quarries for road metal.	
	27.		C.R.E. visited HEBUTERNE defences and left sector of trenches. Adjutant visited DOULLENS.	
	28.		C.R.E. and Adjutant visited AMIENS.	
	29.		C.R.E. went into question of dug-outs for Siege Battery on site and visited BOIS DU WARNIMONT. Adjutant visited ACHEUX.	
	30.		C.R.E. visited new right sector and defences of LA SIGNY FARM. Adjutant visited DOULLENS and woods in neighbourhood,	
	31.		C.R.E. visited HEBUTERNE and investigated question of water supply generally. Adjutant visited BUS and ACHEUX.	

Major R.E.
for C.R.E. 48th Div

121/6598

48th Division

H.Qrs R.E. 48th Division

Vol V

From 1 - 31. 8. 15

CONFIDENTIAL.
****

WAR DIARY

of

48th (South Midland) Divisional Engineers.

(Volume 5.)

From 1st August 1915................................31st August 1915.

Army Form C. 2118.

WAR DIARY
or
INTELLIGENCE SUMMARY.
(Erase heading not required.)

Instructions regarding War Diaries and Intelligence Summaries are contained in F. S. Regs., Part II. and the Staff Manual respectively. Title pages will be prepared in manuscript.

Place	Date 1915	Hour	Summary of Events and Information	Remarks and references to Appendices
AUTHIE.	AUg. 1		Adjutant visited BOIS DU WARNIMONT.	
	2		C.R.E. visited support line trenches with G.O.C., and attended conference in afternoon. Adjutant went to see C.R.E. 4th Division and visited R.E.PARK, ACHEUX, and BUS.	
	3		C.R.E. visited HEBUTERNE Adjutant visited BUS and DOULLENS.	
BUS LES ARTOIS	4		C.R.E. visited HEBUTERNE. Headquarters R.E. removed to BUS LES ARTOIS	
	5th		C.R.E. visited front trenches. Adjutant visited AMIENS.	
	6		C.R.E. accompanied G.O.C. round HEBUTERNE defences. Adjutant and C.R.E. selected hutting sites near BUS LES ARTOIS Adjutant visited DOULLENS	
	7		C.R.E. visited point of junction of 2nd line with C.R.E. 4th Division.	
	8		C.R.E. visited HEBUTERNE	
	9		C.R.E. and G.S.O.1 visited COLINCAMPS & SAILLY.	9th very severe thunderstorm in evening.
	10		C.R.E. visited right sector re flooded trenches. Adjutant visited AMIENS & PICQUIGNY.	
	11		C.R.E. and Adjutant with G.S.O.2 decided arrangements for defence of SAILLY. Adjutant visited DOULLENS.	
	12		C.R.E. visited right sector	
	13		C.R.E. visited HEBUTERNE.	

Army Form C. 2118

WAR DIARY
or
INTELLIGENCE SUMMARY.
(Erase heading not required.)

Instructions regarding War Diaries and Intelligence Summaries are contained in F. S. Regs., Part II. and the Staff Manual respectively. Title pages will be prepared in manuscript.

Place	Date 1915	Hour	Summary of Events and Information	Remarks and references to Appendices
BUS LES ARTOIS.	AUG. 14.		C.R.E. visited support line right sector. Adjutant visited 3rd line, COIGNEUX water supply, and BOIS DU WARNIMONT	
	15.		C.R.E. visited right sector	
	16.		C.R.E. and Adjutant visited HEBUTERNE.	
	17.		C.R.E. and Adjutant visited COLINCAMPS, SAILLY, & BAYENCOURT defences and forward communication trench from SAILLY.	
	18.		C.R.E. and Adjutant visited LA SIGNY and communication trenches on right sector.	
	19.		C.R.E. proceeded on leave. Adjutant attended a conference at Headquarters C.E. 3rd Army.	
	20.		Adjutant visited HEBUTERNE & SAILLY forward communication trench.	
	21.		Adjutant visited SAILLY defences and communication trench.	
	22.		Adjutant visited back communication trench and G.O's.C.shelter	
	23.		Adjutant visited back communication trenches and G.O's.C.shelter.	
	24.		Adjutant visited AMIENS.	
	25.		Adjutant accompanied G.S.O1. and selected Battalion and Headquarters shelters near front line and visited communication trenches.	
	26.		Routine.	

Army Form C. 2118

WAR DIARY
or
INTELLIGENCE SUMMARY.
(Erase heading not required.)

Instructions regarding War Diaries and Intelligence Summaries are contained in F. S. Regs., Part II. and the Staff Manual respectively. Title pages will be prepared in manuscript.

Place	Date 1915.	Hour	Summary of Events and Information	Remarks and references to Appendices
BUS-LES-ARTOIS.	Aug. 27.		Adjt. visited Artillery shelters with S.C., R.A.	
	28.		C.R.E. visited HEBUTERNE and front line. Adjutant visited G.O's C. dugout and back communication trenches.	
	29.		C.R.E. visited BOIS DU WARNIMONT and defences of COURCELLES with G.S.O. 1. Six officers and six N.C.Os of 37th Division arrived for attachment.	
	30.		C.R.E. visited communication trenches with O.C., Pioneer Battalion, and attended tactical exercises. Adjutant visited wood cutting parties.	
	31.		C.R.E. visited battalion Headquarter shelter and communication trenches. Adjutant reconnoitered woods for cutting brushwood and timber, and visited BOIS DU WARNIMONT.	

48th Division

121/6923

HdQrs R.E. 48th Division

Vol VI

Sept. 15.

CONFIDENTIAL.
****

WAR DIARY

of

48th (South Midland) Divisional Engineers.

From 1st September 1915............ to .... 30th September 1915.

(Volume 6.)

Army Form C. 2118.

WAR DIARY
or
INTELLIGENCE SUMMARY.
(Erase heading not required.)

Instructions regarding War Diaries and Intelligence Summaries are contained in F. S. Regs., Part II. and the Staff Manual respectively. Title pages will be prepared in manuscript.

Place	Date 1915.	Hour	Summary of Events and Information	Remarks and references to Appendices
BUS-LES-ARTOIS.	Sept. 1.		C.R.E. visited works at WEST HEBUTERNE. Adjutant visited wood cutting party.	
	2.		C.R.E. visited SAILLY line. Adjutant visited wood cutting party, hut building and LOUVENCOURT re hire of engine. Adjutant visited C.E's office, 3rd Army, BEAUQUESNE.	
	3.		C.R.E. and Adjutant visited new left sector taken over from the French, and LA HAIE. C.R.E. visited SAILLY. Part of 2nd Field Company moved to FONQUEVILLERS.	
	4.		C.R.E. visited front line trenches and JENA. Adjutant visited AMINES. Also reconnoitred a wood for timber cutting.	
	5.		C.R.E. with G.S.O's 1. & 2. visited FONQUEVILLERS defences, also SAILLY line and defences. Adjutant visited huts and WARNIMONT WOOD.	
	6.		C.R.E. visited right sector front line and COURCELLES defences.	
	7.		C.R.E. visited mine in FONQUEVILLERS trenches and BAYENCOURT defences. Adjutant visited DOULLENS, AMIENS and BEAUQUESNE, and water supply at COIGNEUX.	
	8.		C.R.E. visited posts on 7th Corps line. Adjutant visited 3rd line and ROSSIGNOL FARM.	
	9.		C.R.E. visited water supply at COIGNEUX, LARRY trench and COURCELLES defences. Adjutant visited huts. 3rd Field Company moved to ROSSIGNOL.	
	10.		C.R.E. visited HEBUTERNE, SAILLY and COURCELLES defences, and attended conference at Corps Hd. Qrs. at MARIEUX.	
	11.		C.R.E. visited COURCELLES defences and front line trenches right sector. Adjutant with D.A.A. & Q.M.G. visited SAILLY and COURCELLES in reference to winter hutting arrangements.	

1577 Wt.W:10791/1773 50,000 1/15 D. D. & L. A.D.S.S/Forms/C. 2118

Army Form C. 2118

WAR DIARY
or
INTELLIGENCE SUMMARY.

(Erase heading not required.)

Instructions regarding War Diaries and Intelligence Summaries are contained in F. S. Regs., Part II. and the Staff Manual respectively. Title pages will be prepared in manuscript.

Place	Date	Hour	Summary of Events and Information	Remarks and references to Appendices
BUS-LES-ARTOIS.	1915. Sept. 12.		C.R.E. and Adjutant attended G.O's C. Conference. Adjutant with D.A.A. & Q.M.G. visited BAYENCOURT re winter hutting arrangements.	
	13.		C.R.E. visited front line trenches, FONQUEVILLERS and LA HAIE FARM defences. Adjutant visited baths at COUIN and water supply at COIGNEUX.	
	14.		C.R.E. visited right sector front line trenches. C.R.E. and Adjutant visited new keep in right sector trenches.	
	15.	Night.	C.R.E. visited new keep in right sector trenches. Adjutant visited AMIENS.	
	16.		C.R.E. visited right sector communication trenches and new Strong Point.	
	17.		C.R.E. with G.O.C. visited COURCELLES defences and SAILLY line. Adjutant visited BOIS FAYS and BOIS DU WARNIMONT.	
	18.		C.R.E. and Adjutant visited COUIN and COIGNEUX water supply and BAYENCOURT defences. C.R.E. visited support line right sector and WEST HEBUTERNE works. Adjutant visited DOULLENS.	
	19.		C.R.E. visited right sector.	
	20.		C.R.E. visited proposed Tramway line FONQUEVILLERS-HEBUTERNE with Lieut. Briggs of the Rly. Co.	
	21.		C.R.E. visited water supply at COUIN and SAILLY line. Adjutant visited AMIENS.	
	22.		C.R.E. visited right sector and water supply at COUIN. Adjutant visited BOIS DU WARNIMONT, AUTHIE and DOULLENS.	

Army Form C. 2118.

WAR DIARY
or
INTELLIGENCE SUMMARY.
(Erase heading not required.)

Instructions regarding War Diaries and Intelligence Summaries are contained in F. S. Regs., Part II. and the Staff Manual respectively. Title pages will be prepared in manuscript.

Place	Date 1915.	Hour	Summary of Events and Information	Remarks and references to Appendices
BUS-LES-ARTOIS.	Sept. 23.		C.R.E. visited HEBUTERNE and communication trenches right sector.	Wet and cold.
	24.		C.R.E. visited G.O's C. Report Centre.	
	25.		Routine.	
	26.		C.R.E. and Adjutant visited SAILLY.	
	27.		C.R.E. and Adjutant visited communication trenches.	
	28.		C.R.E. visited HEBUTERNE.	
	29.		Routine.	
	30.		C.R.E. visited right sector. Adjutant visited SAILLY and VALLEY ROAD.	

Major R.E.
for C.R.E. 48th Div

12/7381

Hd. Qrs. R.E. 48th Division
Vol VIII
Oct 15

R.E. HEAD QUARTERS
No............
2 NOV 1915
48th. DIVISION.

CONFIDENTIAL.
****

W A R   D I A R Y

o f

48th (South Midland) Divisional Engineers.

(Volume 7.)

From 1st October 1915...................TO..................31st October 1915.

Army Form C. 2118

WAR DIARY
or
INTELLIGENCE SUMMARY.

(Erase heading not required.)

Instructions regarding War Diaries and Intelligence Summaries are contained in F. S. Regs., Part II. and the Staff Manual respectively. Title pages will be prepared in manuscript.

Place	Date 1915.	Hour	Summary of Events and Information	Remarks and references to Appendices
BUS-LES-ARTOIS.	Oct. 1.		C.R.E. visited front line trenches right sector.	
	2.		C.R.E. visited front line trenches right sector.	
	3.		C.R.E. with A.A. & Q.M.G. visited water supply at COUIN and COIGNEUX. C.R.E. and Adjutant visited BOIS FAYS.	
	4.		C.R.E. and Adjutant attended Divisional Conference. C.R.E. visited West HEBUTERNE Defences. Adjutant visited DOULLENS.	
	5.		C.R.E. visited LA HAIE FARM and attended conference with G.O's C. right and left sectors regarding connection between their two sectors and Brigade Reserve Line.	
	6.		C.R.E. visited West HEBUTERNE Defences. Adjutant visited BOIS FAYS and COUIN and COIGNEUX water supplies.	
	7.		C.R.E. and Adjutant sited new trenches in right sector. C.R.E. visited FONQUEVILLERS and HEBUTERNE.	
	8.		C.R.E. visited West HEBUTERNE works and sited trenches right sector. Adjutant visited AMIENS.	
	9.		C.R.E. visited front line right sector. Adjutant visited DOULLENS.	
	10.		C.R.E. visited West HEBUTERNE line. C.R.E. and Adjutant visited ACHEUX, COUIN and COIGNEUX.	
	11.		C.R.E. visited West HEBUTERNE defences. Adjutant visited BOIS FAYS, hutting at ROSSIGNOL and COIGNEUX with D.A.A. & Q.M.G.	

Army Form C. 2118

WAR DIARY
or
INTELLIGENCE SUMMARY.
(Erase heading not required.)

Instructions regarding War Diaries and Intelligence Summaries are contained in F. S. Regs., Part II. and the Staff Manual respectively. Title pages will be prepared in manuscript.

Place	Date 1915.	Hour	Summary of Events and Information	Remarks and references to Appendices
BUS-LES-ARTOIS.	Oct. 12.		C.R.E. visited "K" sector front line. Adjutant visited SAILLY and COIGNEUX.	
	13.		C.R.E. visited Tramway Line right sector with O.C., Railway Detachment, and Battalion Reserve line right sector. Adjutant visited BOIS FAYS and hutting at ROSSIGNOL.	
	14.		C.R.E. and Adjutant visited AMIENS.	
	15.		C.R.E. visited West HEBUTERNE line and Tramway line. Adjutant visited hutting at ROSSIGNOL.	
	16.		C.R.E. visited FONQUEVILLERS. Adjutant visited hutting and inspected new arrangements for water supply at COUIN with A.A. & Q.M.G.	
	17.		Adjutant visited hutting. C.R.E., 4th Division called in respect of arrangements re hutting.	
	18.		C.R.E. and Adjutant visited communications right sector and pivot on WAGRAM.	
	19.		C.R.E. accompanied C.E. round front line trenches, K sector, Tramway line, Brigade Reserve line, hutting and water supply. Adjutant visited BOIS FAYS and hutting.	
	20.		Adjutant visited hutting and COUIN water supply.	
	21.		C.R.E. visited support line right sector and WEST HEBUTERNE works. Adjutant visited hutting BAYENCOURT and ROSSIGNOL.	
	22.		C.R.E. visited G. sector front line and ABLAIN KEEP. Adjutant visited hutting at COUIN, ROSSIGNOL and BAYENCOURT.	

Army Form C. 2118

- 3 -

WAR DIARY
or
INTELLIGENCE SUMMARY.

(Erase heading not required.)

Instructions regarding War Diaries and Intelligence Summaries are contained in F. S. Regs, Part II. and the Staff Manual respectively. Title pages will be prepared in manuscript.

Place	Date 1915	Hour	Summary of Events and Information	Remarks and references to Appendices
BUS-LES-ARTOIS.	Oct. 23.		C.R.E. visited DOULLENS. Adjutant visited hutting at BAYENCOURT, ROSSIGNOL and COUIN with D.A.A. & Q.M.G.	
	24.		C.R.E. visited FONQUEVILLERS, front line left sector and support line. Adjutant visited SAILLY, and hutting at ROSSIGNOL, COUIN and BUS.	
	25.		C.R.E. selected site of observation post with Survey Officer.	
	26.		C.R.E. visited Brigade and Regimental Reserve lines right sector. Adjutant went on leave, and Capt. A.J.M. Wright, 1/2nd S.M. Field Company took over duties of Adjutant during his absence.	
	27.		C.R.E. visited Tramway line HEBUTERNE and FONQUEVILLERS.	
	28.		C.R.E. visited defences of COURCELLES and BAYENCOURT. Actg. Adjutant visited AMIENS.	
	29.		~~C.R.E. visited defences of COURCELLES and BAYENCOURT.~~ C.R.E. visited front line trenches right sector.	
	30.		Routine.	
	31.		C.R.E. visited "H" sector front line trenches.	

A.J. Wright Capt.
~~Major~~ R.E
for C.R.E. 48th Div

48th Division

CONFIDENTIAL.
****

WAR DIARY

of

48th (South Midland) Divisional Engineers.

From 1st November 1915..................to...................30th November 1915.

(Volume 8.)

Army Form C. 2118.

WAR DIARY
or
INTELLIGENCE SUMMARY.
(Erase heading not required.)

Place	Date 1915.	Hour	Summary of Events and Information	Remarks and references to Appendices
BUS-LES-ARTOIS.	Nov. 1.		C.R.E. visited N. Sector, FONQUEVILLERS and Liaison Keeps with 37th Division.	
	2.		C.R.E. accompanied C.E. to inspect BAYENCOURT-LA HAIE Road.	
	3.		C.R.E. visited G. Sector front line trenches and communications. Adjutant visited AMIENS.	
	4.		C.R.E. - Routine. Adjutant visited huts at ROSSIGNOL and SAILLY store.	
	5.		C.R.E. visited L. Sector, FONQUEVILLERS, front line trenches, and Brigade Reserve Line, right sector and Army Observation Post. Adjutant visited hutting and water supply at COIGNEUX and COUIN.	
	6.		C.R.E. attended inspection of experiments with Earth Borer at 3rd Army. Adjutant visited COUIN water supply and DOULLENS.	
	7.		C.R.E. visited G. Sector front line trenches, communication trenches, and Regimental and Brigade Reserve lines.	
	8.		C.R.E. - Routine. Adjutant visited ROSSIGNOL and SAILLY.	
	9.		C.R.E. visited HEBUTERNE, FONQUEVILLERS and Brigade Reserve Line. Adjutant visited BOIS rAYS.	
	10.		C.R.E. visited communications SAILLY-HEBUTERNE. Adjutant visited hutting at ROSSIGNOL.	
	11.		C.R.E. attended Divisional Conference. Adjutant visited huts at AUTHIE and accompanied C.E. round huts at BUS.	
	12.		C.R.E. visited right sector front line trenches. C.R.E. and Adjutant visited MONDICOURT. Adjutant visited COUIN re arrangements for wood cutting.	

Army Form C. 2118.

WAR DIARY
or
INTELLIGENCE SUMMARY.
(Erase heading not required.)

Instructions regarding War Diaries and Intelligence Summaries are contained in F. S. Regs., Part II. and the Staff Manual respectively. Title pages will be prepared in manuscript.

Place	Date 1915.	Hour	Summary of Events and Information	Remarks and references to Appendices
BUS-LES-ARTOIS.	Nov. 13.		C.R.E. visited HEBUTERNE. Adjutant visited wood cutting at CHATEAU WOOD, BUS, COUIN and hutting at ROSSIGNOL and SAILLY.	
	14.		C.R.E. visited BUS defence scheme and G. Sector. Adjutant reconnoitred woods for cutting; visited wood cutting at BUS and COUIN and hutting at ROSSIGNOL and selected site for new workshop near ROSSIGNOL.	
	15.		C.R.E. and Adjutant visited FONQUEVILLERS, SAILLY and BUS wood.	
	16.		C.R.E. visited Regimental Reserve and Brigade Reserve lines right sector and communications. Adjutant visited ST. LEGER & COUIN horse watering place and COIGNEUX water supply; also LOUVENCOURT re billet repairs with D.A.A. & Q.M.G.	
	17.		C.R.E. visited FONQUEVILLERS. Adjutant visited MONDICOURT, DOULLENS and ACHEUX.	
	18.		C.R.E. visited G. Sector front line trenches and communication trenches. Adjutant visited COUIN, ST. LEGER and ROSSIGNOL.	
	19.		C.R.E. made a reconnaissance of proposed new Tramway Line, and visited HEBUTERNE. Adjutant visited ROSSIGNOL and SAILLY.	
	20.		C.R.E. accompanied C.E. round front line trenches H. Sector and communications.	
	21.		C.R.E. visited HEBUTERNE. Adjutant visited SAILLY and ROSSIGNOL. 2 Field Engineers 13th Corps came to see hutting arrangements, etc.	
	22.		C.R.E. visited Brigade and Regimental Reserve Lines, HEBUTERNE and right sector. Adjutant visited ROSSIGNOL.	
	23.		C.R.E. visited FONQUEVILLERS and K. and L. Sectors. Adjutant visited SAILLY.	

Army Form C. 2118

WAR DIARY
or
INTELLIGENCE SUMMARY.
(Erase heading not required.)

Instructions regarding War Diaries and Intelligence Summaries are contained in F.S. Regs., Part II. and the Staff Manual respectively. Title pages will be prepared in manuscript.

Place	Date 1915.	Hour	Summary of Events and Information	Remarks and references to Appendices
BUS-LES-ARTOIS.	Nov. 24.		C.R.E. visited G. Sector front line and communication trenches. Adjutant visited BUS and COUIN woods and ROSSIGNOL.	
	25.		C.R.E. and Adjutant visited ST. LEGER, COUIN, COIGNEUX and SAILLY.	
	25. Night.		Lieut. HUSBANDS and 3 Sappers of the 1st Field Company accompanied Infantry party in an attempt to force their way into the German trenches. The attacking party was divided into two, the Sapper party accompanying one of these. They reached and penetrated the enemy's wire but were held up by wire on parapet; the other party entered the enemy's trenches.	
	26.		C.R.E. and Adjutant visited HEBUTERNE.	
	27.		C.R.E. visited Regimental and Brigade Reserve Lines right sector. Adjutant visited AMIENS.	
	28.		C.R.E. routine. Adjutant visited water supply COUIN and hutting ROSSIGNOL and SAILLY.	
	29.		C.R.E. visited HEBUTERNE.	
	30.		C.R.E. visited FONQUEVILLERS.	

Major R.E.
for C.R.E. 48th Div

C O N F I D E N T I A L.
****

W A R   D A I R Y

of

48th (South Midland) Divisional Engineers.

(Volume 9.)

From 1st December 1915.............to................31st December 1915.

Army Form C. 2118.

WAR DIARY
or
INTELLIGENCE SUMMARY.
(Erase heading not required.)

Instructions regarding War Diaries and Intelligence Summaries are contained in F.S. Regs., Part II. and the Staff Manual respectively. Title pages will be prepared in manuscript.

Place	Date 1915	Hour	Summary of Events and Information	Remarks and references to Appendices
BUS-LES-ARTOIS.	Dec. 1.		C.R.E. visited G. Sector, front line and communication trenches. Adjutant visited SAILLY.	
	2.		C.R.E. Routine. Adjutant attended C.E's office regarding hutting arrangements.	
	3.		C.R.E. visited FONQUEVILLERS, L. and M. Sectors and communications. Adjutant visited SAILLY, COUIN water supply and wood cutting.	
	4.		C.R.E. visited HEBUTERNE and Brigade Reserve line and communications. Adjutant visited SAILLY.	
	5.		C.R.E. and Adjutant with G.S.O.1. visited SAILLY, ROSSIGNOL and COUIN. 202nd Field Company, R.E. arrived and attached for instruction.	
	6.		C.R.E. visited HEBUTERNE and Brigade Reserve line.	
	7.		C.R.E. visited HEBUTERNE, Regimental Reserve line and G. Sector. Adjutant visited AMIENS.	
	8.		C.R.E. visited villages in Divisional area in regard to extra accommodation. Adjutant visited ROSSIGNOL and COUIN.	
	9.		C.R.E. visited SAILLY.	
	10.		C.R.E. attended Corps Conference on hutting at MARIEUX. Adjutant visited COUIN, ROSSIGNOL and SAILLY.	
	11.		C.R.E. Routine. visited HEBUTERNE and FONQUEVILLERS. Adjutant visited SAILLY, ST. LEGER wood and COUIN.	

Army Form C. 2118.

WAR DIARY
or
INTELLIGENCE SUMMARY.
(Erase heading not required.)

Instructions regarding War Diaries and Intelligence Summaries are contained in F. S. Regs., Part II. and the Staff Manual respectively. Title pages will be prepared in manuscript.

Place	Date 1915.	Hour	Summary of Events and Information	Remarks and references to Appendices
BUS-LES-ARTOIS.	Dec. 12.		C.R.E. and Adjutant visited SAILLY.	
	13.		C.R.E. and Adjutant attended conference at Divisional Headquarters. Adjutant visited ST. LEGER wood and COUIN.	
	14.		C.R.E. visited HEBUTERNE.	
	15.		C.R.E. visited FONQUEVILLERS and HEBUTERNE.	
	16.		C.R.E. visited Brigade and Regimental Reserve lines right sector.	
	17.		C.R.E. visited HEBUTERNE and G. Sector. Adjutant visited Garrison Quartermasters at LOUVENCOURT, AUTHIE, ST. LEGER, COUIN, COIGNEUX, BAYENCOURT and COURCELLES.	
	18.		C.R.E. Routine. 202nd Field Company, R.E. left.	
	19.		C.R.E. visited HEBUTERNE & Right Sector. Adjutant tested Schneider Crocodile.	
	20.		C.R.E. visited SAILLY. Adjutant tested Schneider Crocodile on Corps line.	
	21.		C.R.E. visited SAILLY. Adjutant visited AMIENS.	
	22.		C.R.E. visited DOULLENS. Adjutant visited COUIN & ROSSIGNOL FARM.	
	23.		C.R.E. visited HEBUTERNE & Right sector. Adjutant visited COIGNEUX & SAILLY Bridge.	
	24.		C.R.E. Routine.	

Army Form C. 2118.

WAR DIARY
or
INTELLIGENCE SUMMARY.
(Erase heading not required.)

Place	Date 1915.	Hour	Summary of Events and Information	Remarks and references to Appendices
BUS-LES-ARTOIS.	Decr. 24.		Adjutant visited SAILLY.	
	25.		C.R.E. & Adjutant visited HEBUTERNE, ROSSIGNOL Farm & SAILLY.	
	26.		C.R.E. Routine. Adjutant visited ROSSIGNOL FARM.	
	27.		C.R.E. & Adjutant attended lecture on Battle of LOOS at MARIEUX. Adjutant visited SAILLY.	
	28.		C.R.E. attended Corps conference at MARIEUX & visited FONQUEVILLERS & HEBUTERNE. Adjutant visited advanced report centre.	
	29.		C.R.E. Routine. Adjutant visited DOULLENS.	
	30.		C.R.E. & Adjutant attended lecture on battle of LOOS at MARIEUX. Adjutant visited ROSSIGNOL FARM & COUIN.	
	31.		C.R.E. visited HEBUTERNE & Right Sector. Adjutant visited Wood Cutting.	

Major R.E.
for C.R.E. 48th Div.

CONFIDENTIAL.
****

WAR DIARY

of

48th (South Midland) Divisional Engineers.

From 1st January 1916.............to................ 31st January 1916.

(Volume 10.)

Army Form C. 2118.

WAR DIARY
or
INTELLIGENCE SUMMARY.
(Erase heading not required.)

Instructions regarding War Diaries and Intelligence Summaries are contained in F. S. Regs., Part II. and the Staff Manual respectively. Title pages will be prepared in manuscript.

Place	Date	Hour	Summary of Events and Information	Remarks and references to Appendices
BUS-LES-ARTOIS.	Jan.			
	1.		C.R.E. Routine. Adjutant, Routine.	
	2.		C.R.E. & Adjutant visited HEBUTERNE & SAILLY.	
	3.		C.R.E. & Adjutant visited AMIENS with G.S.O.2	
	4.		Routine.	
	5.		C.R.E. visited HEBUTERNE. Adjutant explained working of R.E.Stores etc. to party of Officers visiting Div. Hd. Qrs.	
	6.		C.R.E. & Adjutant visited SAILLY & FONQUEVILLERS with G.S.O.1.	
	7.		C.R.E. visited SAILLY & selected site for new R.E. Store at COURCELLES.	
	8.		C.R.E. visited HEBUTERNE & Right Sector. Adjutant visited COURCELLES, re new Store, SAILLY & ROSSIGNOL.	
	9.		C.R.E. visited HEBUTERNE & FONQUEVILLERS, & Brigade Reserve Line.	
	10.		Routine.	
	11.		C.R.E. visited FONQUEVILLERS.	
	12.		C.R.E. visited FONQUEVILLERS with G.O.C.	
	13.		C.R.E. visited COURCELLES. Adjutant visited ROSSIGNOL & COIGNEUX Wood. Major A.D.Walker joined as Adjutant vice Major O.G.Brandon to 14th Corps.	
	14.		C.R.E. visited HEBUTERNE & FONQUEVILLERS with expert from Camouflage Section, and selected Artillery Observation Posts.	

Army Form C. 2118.

WAR DIARY
or
INTELLIGENCE SUMMARY.
(Erase heading not required.)

Instructions regarding War Diaries and Intelligence Summaries are contained in F. S. Regs., Part II. and the Staff Manual respectively. Title pages will be prepared in manuscript.

Place	Date	Hour	Summary of Events and Information	Remarks and references to Appendices
BUS-LES-ARTOIS.	Jan. 14.		Adjutant visited COURCELLES & SAILLY.	
	15.		C.R.E. visited FONQUEVILLERS	
	16.		Adjutant visited AMIENS.	
	17.		C.R.E. visited SAILLY & COURCELLES Adjutant visited BEAUSSART & COURCELLES.	
	18.		C.R.E. visited HEBUTERNE, ROSSIGNOL & SAILLY.	
	19.		Major O.G.Brandon left for duty with 14th Corps. C.R.E. visited with C.E. HEBUTERNE & FONQUEVILLERS. Adjutant visited BEAUSSART & COURCELLES	
	20.		C.R.E. Routine. Adjutant visited AMIENS.	
	21.		C.R.E. visited HEBUTERNE and right sector. Adjutant visited COURCELLES.	
	22.		C.R.E. and Adjutant visited COURCELLES.	
	23.		C.R.E. visited HEBUTERNE and right sector. Adjutant visited DOULLENS and MONDICOURT.	
	24.		C.R.E. and Adjutant visited BEAUSSART, COURCELLES, SAILLY and COIGNEUX.	
	25.		C.R.E. visited FONQUEVILLERS and Brigade Reserve Line.	
			Adjutant visited HEBUTERNE and AMIENS.	

Army Form C. 2118.

WAR DIARY
or
INTELLIGENCE SUMMARY.
(Erase heading not required.)

Instructions regarding War Diaries and Intelligence Summaries are contained in F. S. Regs., Part II. and the Staff Manual respectively. Title pages will be prepared in manuscript.

Place	Date 1916-	Hour	Summary of Events and Information	Remarks and references to Appendices
BUS-LES-ARTOIS.	Jan. 26.		C.R.E. and Adjutant with G.O.C. visited FONQUEVILLERS and HEBUTERNE.	
	27.		C.R.E. visited HEBUTERNE. Adjutant visited COURCELLES.	
	28.		Adjutant visited MONDICOURT and DOULLENS.	
	29.		C.R.E. visited HEBUTERNE and right sector, Adjutant visited AMIENS.	
	30.		C.R.E. visited HEBUTERNE. Adjutant visited COURCELLES and ROSSIGNOL.	
	31.		C.R.E. visited HEBUTERNE. Adjutant visited BERTRANCOURT.	

Major R.E.
for C.R.E. 48th Div.

CONFIDENTIAL.
****

WAR DIARY

of

48th (South Midland) Divisional Engineers.

From 1st February 1916................to...........29th February 1916.

Army Form C. 2118

WAR DIARY
or
INTELLIGENCE SUMMARY
(Erase heading not required.)

Instructions regarding War Diaries and Intelligence Summaries are contained in F. S. Regs., Part II. and the Staff Manual respectively. Title Pages will be prepared in manuscript.

Place	Date 1916. FEB.	Hour	Summary of Events and Information	Remarks and references to Appendices
BUS-LES-ARTOIS.	1		C.R.E. Routine. Adjutant visited MARIEUX, COIGNEUX, COUIN, ST.LEGER.	
	2		C.R.E. & Adjutant visited FONQUEVILLERS & SAILLY.	
	3		C.R.E. Visited HEBUTERNE, G & L Sectors Adjutant visited COURCELLES & ROSSIGNOL.	
	4		C.R.E. visited BIENVILLERS, HANNESCAMPS & Front line 37th Divn. Right Sector. Adjutant visited ROSSIGNOL & MONDICOURT.	
	5		C.R.E. visited AMIENS. Adjutant visited PAS, BIENVILLERS, MONDICOURT, & DOULLENS.	
	6		C.R.E. Routine. Adjutant visited BETRANCOURT & COLINCAMPS.	
	7		C.R.E. Routine. Adjutant visited LOUVENCOURT, AUTHIE, & ROSSIGNOL. 9th Field Company R.E. attached for	
	8		C.R.E. Routine. Adjutant visited AMIENS.	
	9		C.R.E. visited HEBUTERNE & FONQUEVILLERS and selected Artillery Observation Posts with C.R.A. Adjutant visited LOUVENCOURT & BETRANCOURT.	
	10		C.R.E. visited PAS & SOUASTRE. Adjutant, Routine. 3 sections of 1st. Field Coy. moved from ROSSIGNOL to HEBUTERNE and 3 sections of the 3rd Field Company from HEBUTERNE to ROSSIGNOL.	

Army Form C. 2118

WAR DIARY
or
INTELLIGENCE SUMMARY
(Erase heading not required.)

Instructions regarding War Diaries and Intelligence Summaries are contained in F.S. Regs., Part II. and the Staff Manual respectively. Title Pages will be prepared in manuscript.

Place	Date 1916	Hour	Summary of Events and Information	Remarks and references to Appendices
BUS-LES-ARTOIS.	FEB. 11		C.R.E. visited COLINCAMPS & HEBUTERNE Adjutant visited COURCELLES & BEAUSSART.	
	12		C.R.E. & Adjutant visited COURCELLES & SAILLY.	
	13		C.R.E. visited COLINCAMPS & SUCRERIE. Adjutant visited COLINCAMPS & COURCELLES.	
	14		C.R.E. Routine. Adjutant visited AMIENS. 3 sections of 3rd Field Coy. moved to BIENVILLERS from ROSSIGNOL and one section (Headquarters) and Mounted section to SOUASTRE.	
	15		C.R.E. visited PAS, SOUASTRE, BIENVILLERS, & HEBUTERNE. Adjutant visited COURCELLES. 1 Section, 2nd Field Coy. moved from SAILLY to FONQUEVILLERS and Headquarters moved from SAILLY to ROSSIGNOL.	
	16		C.R.E. Routine. Adjutant visited ROSSIGNOL.	
	17		C.R.E. & Adjutant visited SOUASTRE, FONQUEVILLERS, & SAILLY.	
	18		C.R.E. visited COURCELLES & COLINCAMPS. Adjutant Routine.	
	19		C.R.E. Routine. Adjutant visited AMIENS.	
	20		C.R.E. visited HEBUTERNE, G. Sector. Adjutant visited AUTHIE & ROSSIGNOL FARM.	

Army Form C. 2118

WAR DIARY
or
INTELLIGENCE SUMMARY
(Erase heading not required.)

Instructions regarding War Diaries and Intelligence Summaries are contained in F. S. Regs., Part II. and the Staff Manual respectively. Title Pages will be prepared in manuscript.

Place	Date 1916	Hour	Summary of Events and Information	Remarks and references to Appendices
BUS-LES-ARTOIS.	FEB. 21		C.R.E. visited BIENVILLERS, FONQUEVILLERS & HANNESCAMPS. Adjutant routine.	
	22		C.R.E. routine. Adjutant visited AMIENS.	
	23		C.R.E. visited COLINCAMPS. Adjutant visited COLINCAMPS.	
	24		C.R.E. visited FONQUEVILLERS. Adjutant visited BERTRANCOURT.	
	25		C.R.E. visited HEBUTERNE Adjutant routine.	
	26		C.R.E. & Adjutant routine.	
	27		C.R.E. visited FONQUEVILLERS & ROSSIGNOL FARM. Adjutant " "	
	28		C.R.E. & Adjutant routine.	
	29		C.R.E. routine. Adjutant visited LOUVENCOURT & AUTHIE.	

Major R.E.
for C.R.E. 48th Div.

R.E. HEAD QUARTERS
No.4.A.A.R.E.
3 1 MAR 1916
48th DIVISION.

Vol XII

C O N F I D E N T I A L.
****

W A R   D I A R Y

of

48th (South Midland) Divisional Engineers.

From 1st March 1916................to................31st March 1916.

Army Form C. 2118.

WAR DIARY
or
INTELLIGENCE SUMMARY.
(Erase heading not required.)

- 2 -

Instructions regarding War Diaries and Intelligence Summaries are contained in F. S. Regs., Part II. and the Staff Manual respectively. Title pages will be prepared in manuscript.

Place	Date	Hour	Summary of Events and Information	Remarks and references to Appendices
HEM.	1916. May 18.		HEM.	
	19.		HEM.	
	20.		C.R.E. and Adjutant visited HEBUTERNE.	
	21.		At HEM.	
	22.		C.R.E. and Adjutant visited HEBUTERNE.	
	23.		C.R.E. attended Corps Conference and afterwards visited HEBUTERNE.	
	24-26.		At HEM.	
	27.		C.R.E. and Adjutant visited SAILLY.	
	28.		R.E. Headquarters and 1/2nd S.M. Field Co.R.E. moved from HEM to COUIN and ROSSIGNOL respectively.	
	29.		C.R.E. - Routine. Adjutant visited FAMECHON and COIGNEUX.	
	30.		C.R.E. - Routine. Adjutant visited AMIENS.	
	31.		C.R.E. -& Adjutant attended demonstration of Hydraulic Jack Pipe Forcing Jack at RIBEMONT.	

Major R.E.
for C.R.E. 48th Div

Army Form C. 2118

WAR DIARY
or
INTELLIGENCE SUMMARY

(Erase heading not required.)

Instructions regarding War Diaries and Intelligence Summaries are contained in F.S. Regs., Part II. and the Staff Manual respectively. Title Pages will be prepared in manuscript.

Place	Date 1916.	Hour	Summary of Events and Information	Remarks and references to Appendices
BUS-LES-ARTOIS.	Mar.			
	1		C.R.E. visited HEBUTERNE & H.Sector of COLINCAMPS. Adjutant visited COLINCAMPS, COURCELLES, & ROSSIGNOL.	
	2		C.R.E., Routine. Adjutant visited AUTHIE & LUCHEUX WOODS.	
	3		C.R.E. visited HEBUTERNE & FONQUEVILLERS. Adjutant visited FONQUEVILLERS.	
	4		C.R.E. visited HEBUTERNE & COLINCAMPS with G.O.C. Adjutant visited AMIENS & HEBUTERNE.	
	5		C.R.E. visited FONQUEVILLERS, Adjutant, Routine.	
	6		C.R.E., Routine, Adjutant, Routine.	
	7		C.R.E. visited FONQUEVILLERS, Adjutant visited AMIENS.	
	8		C.R.E. visited SAILLY. Adjutant visited SOUASTRE.	
	9		C.R.E. visited HEBUTERNE. Adjutant, Routine.	
	10		C.R.E., Routine, Adjutant visited ROSSIGNOL.	
	11		C.R.E., Routine, Adjutant, Routine.	

Army Form C. 2118

WAR DIARY
or
INTELLIGENCE SUMMARY
(Erase heading not required.)

Instructions regarding War Diaries and Intelligence Summaries are contained in F. S. Regs., Part II. and the Staff Manual respectively. Title Pages will be prepared in manuscript.

Place	Date 1916.	Hour	Summary of Events and Information	Remarks and references to Appendices
BUS-LES-ARTOIS.	March. 12		C.R.E., visited COLINCAMPS, HEBUTERNE & FONQUEVILLERS. Adjutant visited ROSSIGNOL.	
	13		C.R.E. visited roads at LOUVENCOURT, AUTHIE, & COIGNEUX. Adjutant, ditto. ditto.	
	14		C.R.E., Routine. Adjutant visited AMIENS.	
	15		C.R.E., Routine. Adjutant visited BAYENCOURT.	
	16		C.R.E. visited COLINCAMPS, Adjutant visited MONDICOURT.	
	17		C.R.E. visited HEBUTERNE & COLINCAMPS with Major Briggs R.E. ROGERS Adjutant visited COUIN.	
	18		C.R.E. & Adjutant visited FONQUEVILLERS & HEBUTERNE.	
	19		C.R.E., Routine, Adjutant visited COUIN.	
	20		C.R.E.,Routine, Adjutant visited COUIN & ROSSIGNOL.	
	21		C.R.E. went on leave, Adjutant visited COUIN.	
	22		Adjutant visited COUIN.	

Army Form C. 2118

WAR DIARY
or
INTELLIGENCE SUMMARY
(Erase heading not required.)

Instructions regarding War Diaries and Intelligence Summaries are contained in F. S. Regs., Part II. and the Staff Manual respectively. Title Pages will be prepared in manuscript.

Place	Date 1916	Hour	Summary of Events and Information	Remarks and references to Appendices
BUS-LES-ARTOIS.	Mar. 23		Adjutant attended G.O.C's conference at SAILLY.	
	24		Adjutant visited COUIN & ROSSIGNOL.	
	25		Adjutant visited AMIENS.	
	26		Headquarters R.E. moved to COUIN.	
	27		Adjutant visited COLINCAMPS & SAILLY with C.E. 8th Corps.	
	28		Adjutant attended G.O.C's conference at Advanced Headquarters.	
	28		Adjutant visited COIGNEUX, MARIEUX, ACHEUX, & BERTRANCOURT.	
	29		Adjutant visited BUS.	
	30		Adjutant, Routine. C.R.E. returned from leave.	
	31	c	C.R.E. visited SAILLY & HEBUTERNE. Adjutant, Routine.	

Major R.E.
for C.R.E. 48th Div

30 APR 1916
48th DIVISION.

C O N F I D E N T I A L.
****

W A R D I A R Y

of

48th (South Midland) Divisional Engineers.

From 1st April 1916..................to.............30th April 1916,

Volume XIII

Army Form C. 2118.

WAR DIARY
or
INTELLIGENCE SUMMARY.
(Erase heading not required.)

Instructions regarding War Diaries and Intelligence Summaries are contained in F. S. Regs., Part II. and the Staff Manual respectively. Title pages will be prepared in manuscript.

Place	Date	Hour	Summary of Events and Information	Remarks and references to Appendices
COUIN.	1916. April. 1.		C.R.E. visited COLINCAMPS and HEBUTERNE. Adjutant visited AUTHIE.	
	2.		C.R.E. Routine.	
	3.		C.R.E. and Adjt. attended G.O's C. Conference. 3rd Field Co. R.E. moved from COLINCAMPS and COURCELLES to SAILLY and HEBUTERNE.	
	4.		C.R.E. visited HEBUTERNE. Adjutant visited COIGNEUX and SOUASTRE. C.R.E. and Adjt. attended G.O's C. Conference.	
	5.		C.R.E. visited HEBUTERNE with G.O.C. Adjutant visited AMIENS.	
	6.		C.R.E. and Adjt. attended G.O's C. Conference.	
	7.		C.R.E. visited HEBUTERNE. Adjutant visited COIGNEUX.	
	8.		C.R.E. and Adjutant attended G.O's C. Conference.	
	9.		C.R.E. visited HEBUTERNE. Adjutant visited ROSSIGNOL.	
	10.		C.R.E. visited FONQUEVILLERS and HEBUTERNE. Adjutant visited BAYENCOURT and COIGNEUX.	
	11.		C.R.E. and Adjt. attended G.O's C. Conference.	

Army Form C. 2118.

WAR DIARY
or
INTELLIGENCE SUMMARY.
(Erase heading not required.)

Place	Date	Hour	Summary of Events and Information	Remarks and references to Appendices
COUIN.	1916. April 12.		C.R.E. Routine. Major A.D. Walker, R.E. went on leave. 2nd Lieut. E.A. Sainsbury, R.E. took on duties as Adjutant during Major Walker's absence.	
	13.		C.R.E. visited HEBUTERNE. Adjutant visited COIGNEUX.	
	14.		C.R.E. and Adjt. attended G.O's C. Conference.	
	15.		C.R.E. attended G.O's C. Conference.	
	16.		C.R.E. visited HEBUTERNE.	
	17.		C.R.E. Routine. Adjutant visited AMIENS.	
	18.		C.R.E. visited HEBUTERNE with Chief Engineer. C.R.E. and Adjt. attended G.O's C. Conference.	
	19.		C.R.E. attended Conference at 8th Corps Hd. Qrs.	
	20.		C.R.E. visited HEBUTERNE. Major A.D. Walker, R.E. returned from leave.	
	21.		C.R.E. visited HEBUTERNE. C.R.E. and Adjt. attended G.O's C. Conference.	
	22.		C.R.E. Routine. Adjutant visited COURCELLES, ACHEUX and LOUVENCOURT.	
	23.		C.R.E. visited HEBUTERNE. Adjutant attended G.O's C. Conference.	

Army Form C. 2118.

WAR DIARY
or
INTELLIGENCE SUMMARY.
(Erase heading not required.)

Instructions regarding War Diaries and Intelligence Summaries are contained in F. S. Regs., Part II. and the Staff Manual respectively. Title pages will be prepared in manuscript.

Place	Date	Hour	Summary of Events and Information	Remarks and references to Appendices
COUIN.	1916. April 24.		C.R.E. and Adjt. attended G.O's C. Conference.	
	25.		C.R.E. visited HEBUTERNE with C.R.A. C.R.E. attended G.O's C. Conference. Adjutant visited AMIENS.	
	26.		C.R.E./attended G.O's C. Conference and Adjt.	
	27.		C.R.E. Routine. Adjutant visited COIGNEUX and SAILLY.	
	28.		C.R.E. visited VALHEUREUX. Adjutant visited AUTHIE.	
	29.		Routine.	
	30.		C.R.E. visited HEBUTERNE with Chief Engineer. Adjutant visited SOUASTRE.	

[signature]

Major R.E.
for C.R.E. 48th Div

R.E. HEAD QUARTERS
No..........
3 1 MAY 1916
48th DIVISION.

C O N F I D E N T I A L
****

W A R   D I A R Y

o f

48th (South Midland) Divisional Engineers.

From 1st May 1916............to.............31st May 1916.

(Volume No.) 14

Army Form C. 2118.

WAR DIARY
or
INTELLIGENCE SUMMARY.
(Erase heading not required.)

Instructions regarding War Diaries and Intelligence Summaries are contained in F. S. Regs., Part II. and the Staff Manual respectively. Title pages will be prepared in manuscript.

Place	Date	Hour	Summary of Events and Information	Remarks and references to Appendices
COUIN.	1916. May. 1.		C.R.E. - Routine. Adjutant visited AUTHIE.	
	2.		C.R.E. - Routine. Adjutant visited HEM.	
	3.		C.R.E. - Routine. Adjutant visited COIGNEUX. 2/1st S.M. Field Co. R.E. moved from HEBUTERNE and SAILLY to ROSSIGNOL.	
	4.		C.R.E. and Adjutant visited HEM. 2/1st S.M. Field Co.R.E. moved from ROSSIGNOL to HEM,	
	5.		C.R.E. visited FONQUEVILLERS and HEBUTERNE. 1/2nd S.M. Field Co.R.E. moved from FONQUEVILLERS to ROSSIGNOL.	
	6.		C.R.E. - Routine. Adjutant visited COIGNEUX. 1/2nd S.M. Field Co.R.E. moved from ROSSIGNOL to HEM.	
	7.		R.E. Headquarters moved to HEM from COUIN.	
	8-13		At HEM.	
	10.		Adjutant visited HEBUTERNE.	
	13.		C.R.E. and Adjutant visited HEBUTERNE.	
	14.		At HEM.	
	15.		2/1st S.M. Field Co.R.E. moved from HEM to ROSSIGNOL.	
	16.		1/1st S.M. Field Co.R.E. moved from ROSSIGNOL to HEM.	
	17.		C.R.E. and Adjutant visited HEBUTERNE.	

1577 Wt.W10791/1773 500,000 1/15 D. D. & L. A.D.S.S./Forms/C. 2118.

C O N F I D E N T I A L.
* * * * * * * * * *
W A R   D I A R Y

of

48th (South Midland) Divisional Engineers.

(Volume 13.)

From 1st June 1916................to................30th June 1916.

Army Form C. 2118.

WAR DIARY
or
INTELLIGENCE SUMMARY.
(Erase heading not required.)

Instructions regarding War Diaries and Intelligence Summaries are contained in F. S. Regs., Part II. and the Staff Manual respectively. Title pages will be prepared in manuscript.

Place	Date	Hour	Summary of Events and Information	Remarks and references to Appendices
COUIN.	1916. June.			
	1.		C.R.E. - Routine. Adjutant visited COIGNEUX and FAMECHON.	
	2.		C.R.E. - Routine. Adjutant visited HEBUTERNE, SAILLY and COIGNEUX. 2/1st S.M. Field Co. R.E. moved to HEM.from ROSSIGNOL. 1/1st S.M. Field Co. R.E. moved from HEM to SAILLY.	
	3.		C.R.E. went on leave. Adjutant visited HEBUTERNE with Chief Engineer.	
	4.		Adjutant visited SAILLY, COURCELLES and COIGNEUX.	
	5.		Adjutant visited SAILLY and HEBUTERNE with A.D.M.S. to settle site of A.D.S. and with Signal officer re Signalling Observation Post.	
	6.		Adjutant visited SAILLY.	
	7.		Adjutant visited COIGNEUX.	
	8.		Adjutant visited SAILLY and attended Divisional Exercise.	
	9.		do.	
	10.		Adjutant visited HEBUTERNE.	
	11.		Adjutant visited HEBUTERNE. 2/1st S.M. Field Co. R.E. Hd. Qrs. and 2 sections moved from HEM to ROSSIGNOL and one section moved from HEM to LOUVENCOURT.	
	12.		Adjutant visited COIGNEUX and SAILLY.	
	13.		do. do.	

1577 Wt.W10791/1773 500,000 1/15 D. D. & L. A.D.S.S./Forms/C. 2118.

Army Form C. 2118.

WAR DIARY
or
INTELLIGENCE SUMMARY.
(Erase heading not required.)

Instructions regarding War Diaries and Intelligence Summaries are contained in F. S. Regs., Part II. and the Staff Manual respectively. Title pages will be prepared in manuscript.

Place	Date	Hour	Summary of Events and Information	Remarks and references to Appendices
COUIN.	1916. June			
	14.		Adjutant visited HEBUTERNE.	
	15.		Adjutant visited HEBUTERNE.	
	16.		Adjutant visited HEBUTERNE and SAILLY.	
	17.		Adjutant visited COIGNEUX.	
	18.		Adjutant visited HEBUTERNE.	
	19.		ditto.	
	20.		ditto.	
	21.		Adjutant visited HEBUTERNE. One section 2/1st S.M. Field Co. R.E. moved from LOUVENCOURT to ROSSIGNOL.	
	22.		Adjutant visited the DELL, SAILLY.	
	23.		Adjutant visited SAILLY.	
	24.		Adjutant visited HEBUTERNE.	
	25.		Adjutant visited MAILLY MAILLET.	
	26.		Adjutant visited AMIENS. C.R.E. returned.	
	27.		C.R.E. and Adjutant visited HEBUTERNE.	
	28.		C.R.E. and Adjutant visited VARENNES and MARIEUX.	
	29.		C.R.E. and Adjutant visited BERTRANCOURT and MAILLY MAILLET.	
	30.		Routine.	

Sawley
Major R.E.
for C.R.E. 48th Div.

CONFIDENTIAL.
****
WAR DIARY

of

48th (South Midland) Divisional Engineers.

From 1st July 1916................to..................31st July 1916.

(Volume 10.)

Army Form C. 2118.

WAR DIARY
or
INTELLIGENCE SUMMARY.
(Erase heading not required.)

Instructions regarding War Diaries and Intelligence Summaries are contained in F. S. Regs., Part II. and the Staff Manual respectively. Title pages will be prepared in manuscript.

Place	Date	Hour	Summary of Events and Information	Remarks and references to Appendices
COUIN.	1916. July 1.		C.R.E., Adjt. and Advanced R.E. Hd. Qrs. moved from COUIN to MAILLY MAILLET. 1/1st S.M. Field Co. and 2/1st S.M. Field Company moved to MAILLY MAILLET.	
	2.		C.R.E., reconnoitred Brigade Reserve Line. Adjutant visited ENGELBERMER.	
	3.		C.R.E., Adjt. and Advanced R.E. Hd. Qrs. returned from MAILLY MAILLET to COUIN. 1/1st S.M. Field Co. and 2/1st S.M. Field Co. moved from MAILLY MAILLET to SAILLY and ROSSIGNOL respectively.	
	4.		C.R.E. and Adjutant visited BUS-LES-ARTOIS & COURCELLES. Two sections 2/1st S.M. Field Company moved to COLINCAMPS.	
	5.		C.R.E. visited COLINCAMPS. Adjutant visited MERICOURT and VARENNES. Hd. Qrs. and 2 sections 2/1st S.M. Field Company moved to COURCELLES. 1/2nd S.M. Field Company moved to ROSSIGNOL.	
	6.		C.R.E. visited COURCELLES and BEAUSSART. Adjutant visited BEAUSSART.	
	7.		C.R.E. visited COLINCAMPS and trenches.	
	8.		C.R.E. visited SAILLY line. Adjutant visited COLINCAMPS.	
	9.		C.R.E. visited COLINCAMPS sector.	
	10.		C.R.E. - Routine. Adjutant visited AMIENS.	
	11.		C.R.E. visited COLINCAMPS and THE DELL.	

1577 Wt. W10791/1773 50,000 1/15 D. D. & L. A.D.S.S./Forms/C. 2118.

Army Form C. 2118.

WAR DIARY
or
INTELLIGENCE SUMMARY.
(Erase heading not required.)

Instructions regarding War Diaries and Intelligence Summaries are contained in F. S. Regs., Part II. and the Staff Manual respectively. Title pages will be prepared in manuscript.

Place	Date	Hour	Summary of Events and Information	Remarks and references to Appendices
COUIN.	1916. July. 12.		C.R.E. visited COURCELLES and COLINCAMPS. Adjutant visited EUSTON and COLINCAMPS.	
	13.		Routine.	
	14.		1/2nd S.M. Field Co. R.E. moved from ROSSIGNOL to ALBERT.	
	15.		C.R.E. moved from COUIN to BOUZINCOURT. 1/1st S.M. Field Co. R.E. moved from SAILLY to BOUZINCOURT. 2/1st S.M. Field Co. R.E. moved from COURCELLES to BOUZINCOURT.	
	16.		R.E. Hd. Qrs. moved from COUIN to BOUZINCOURT.	
	17-27.		See attached summaries of work.	
	28-29.		R.E. Hd. Qrs. moved from BOUZINCOURT to DOMQUEUR. 1/1st and 2/1st S.M. Field Co. R.E. moved to DOMQUEUR. 1/2nd S.M. Field Co. R.E. moved to LE MENAGE.	
DOMQUEUR.	30.		At DOMQUEUR.	
	31.		do.	

Major R.E.
for C.R.E. 48th Div

SUMMARY OF ENGINEER AND PIONEER WORK CARRIED OUT BY
48th DIVISION IN THE OVILLERS - LA BOISSELLE AREA
FROM 16-7-16 to 27-7-16.

****

C.R.E. took over line on evening 16-7-16. Northern limit of line as taken over:-

Sap No.5 - 09 - 39 - 69 - 67 - 18 - 31 - 70 - 46 - 90 - along BAPAUME ROAD to 66.

Northern limit of line on 27-7-16:-

37 - 88 - 47 - 39 - 79 - 11 - 54 - 89 - 31 (junction with ANZAC CORPS)

WORK. The R.E. parties attached to Infantry Brigades followed close behind the Infantry in their advance along the trenches forming strong points at all important trench junctions, straightening trenches, inserting bomb stops, and improving communications trenches. As the advance progressed two communications were made across "NO MAN'S" land an inner defence line 11 - 44 - 78 - 46 was made and Keeps constructed at LA BOISSELLE and OVILLERS: both the defence line and the Keeps were reinforced with supporting points.

New trenches were dug as follows:-

```
X.2.d.47 - X.3.c.25
X.2.d.44 - X.3.c.02
X.3.c.93 - X.3.d.28
X.3.d.14 - X.3.d.63
X.9.b.57 - X.9.b.99
X.3.d.30 - X.3.d.41 )
X.9.b.58 - X.3.d.80 ) Partially dug.
X.9.b.88 - X.3.d.84 )
X.9.b.66 - X.8.d.70 )
```

ROADS. Repairs carried out to both the BAPAUME and the OVILLERS roads the latter being made passable up to X.8.b.78.

A fair weather track to enable Infantry to go from BOUZINCOURT to AVELUY out of observation of the enemy.

WATER SUPPLY. 4 wells in OVILLERS and LA BOISSELLE have been opened up, water analysed, and installation of water drawing arrangements has been started.

TRAMWAYS. Working repairs and extension have been carried out by the Pioneers.

Major R.E.
for C R.E. 48th Div.

27-6-16.

48th DIVISION.

SUMMARY OF ENGINEER WORK EXECUTED DURING 24 HOURS ENDING 3 a.m. 27. 7. 16.

TRENCHES. X.3.c.7.9. - X.3.b.5.4.   Cleaned and deepened.

X.2.d.4.7. - X.3.c.6.3.   Completed throughout as fire trench.

X.3.d.1.4. - X.3.d.6.4.   Ordered to be Completed as fire trench. but work could not be done on account of gas.

STRONG POINTS.   X.3.c.7.9.   Firebayed, traversed and wired.

X.3.b.8.9.   Provided with firebays and bombstop.

SUPPORT LINE.   Trench 88 - 71 dug through and continued to 61.

71 - 59 deepened and widened.

OVILLERS KEEP   N.E. to S.E. supporting points practically completed with firebays, wiring and communication trenches.

GENERAL.   Work last night was much hampered by gas shells, rifle grenades, etc.   1. officer and 37 O.R. of 1/1st S. M. Field CO. R.E. have been detained by Ambulance suffering from gassing.

Major R.E.
For C.R.E., 48th Division.

6.45 a.m.
27. 7. 16.

48th DIVISION.

SUMMARY OF ENGINEER WORK EXECUTED DURING 24 HOURS ENDING 3-0 a.m. 28-7-16

STRONG POINTS.   X.3.b.11 - 54 - 89 under construction.

INNER DEFENCE LINE.   The gap still left in this line from X.2.c.71 - 92 was completed.

COMMUNICATION TRENCHES.   X.9.c.28 - X.3.c.93 new trench completed to depth of about 3' (3'-9" in places)

X.3.d.0.2 - X.3.d.7.9. - deepened widened and revetted in places.

WIRING.   X.2.d.47 - 3.c.38 - 800 yards wired with double apron and 2 rows concertina wire.

GENERAL.   1. Streets 1 - 4 and Avenues 1 - 6 labelled with boards at ends and all crossings.

2. Survey of dug-outs in OVILLERS and BOISSELLE completed

Major R.E.
for C.R.E. 48th Div.

6-45 a.m.
28-7-16.

48th DIVISION.

SUMMARY OF ENGINEER WORK EXECUTED DURING 24 HOURS ENDING 3. a.m.- 26-7-16.

STRONG POINTS. X.3.b.11) Further improved with extra wiring and
X.3.b.81) machine gun platforms.

X.3.b.54 - started.

X.3.d.28 -   do.

X.3.c.79 - 45 yards of trench N.W. of this point deepened and cleaned: trench straightened and loophole traverse made to commande same.

FIRE TRENCH. X.9.b.66 - X.3.c.93 to be cleaned out.

NEW TRENCH. Fire trenches X.3.c.26 extended to join trench between X.3.c.02 - 79.

Trenches dug previous night improved.

COMMUNICATIONS. X.6.b.76 - X.3.c.82 trench cleared and deepened (complete except for last 20 yards).

WALTNEY tunnel connected up to assembly trench in old "No Man's land".

INNER DEFENCE LINE. X.2.c.88 - X.2.a.61 - opened up to within 20 yards of 61 (trench practically non existent before).

OVILLERS KEEP. (a) S.E. supporting point 80 yards of trench cleared - 3 new firebays made and 2 M.G. positions made - partly wired - approach made to good mined dug-out in area of S.P.

(b) E. supporting point - 120 yards trench cleared and deepened - 4 firebays and 1 M.G. position firing E. and N.E. made - approaches made to 1 dug-out and one good cellar in area of S.P. - 1 bay high wire fence with double apron made on E. face - 110 yards new communication trench dug to connect with outer keep.

Major R.E.
for C.R.E. 48th Div

8-30 a.m.

26-7-16.

48th DIVISION.

SUMMARY OF ENGINEERING WORK EXECUTED DURING 24 HOURS ENDING 3 a.m. 25-7-16.

TRENCHES.
from X.3.c.0.6½. for 200 yards W. ⎫ dug 3'x3' with 1'6"
                                                    ⎬ parapet: and completed
X.3.c.0.6½ for 100 yards S.E. ⎭ with traverses and fire trench.

X.3.c.9.3. - X.3.d.2.8.   deepened to 5'

X.8.b.7.1. - X.8.b.7.5.   repaired and deepened.

X.8.b.7.5. - X.8.b.6.5.   firebayed and traversed.

X.8.b.7.6. - X.3.c.7.9.   repaired and improved.

STRONG POINTS.
at X.3.c.1.1. wired and furnished with two T's for 8 to 12 rifles each.

at X.3.c.8.1. prepared for 14 rifles: wired and dug.

ROAD.
BAPAUME ROAD: shell holes filled up to 14.b.1.6.

                                                                                            C.R.E.   Major R.E.,
                                                                          for/48th Division

6-10 a.m.

25-7-16.

48th DIVISION.

SUMMARY OF ENGINEER WORK EXECUTED DURING 24 HOURS ENDING 3-0 a.m., - 24-7-16.

Consolodation of Line.

X.2.c.11 - 24 - 37 - 220 yds. cleaned and deepened.
X.2.d.02 - 10 - 44 - 160 yds.   ditto.
X.2.d.44 - 47 - 100 yds.   ditto.
X.8.b.78 - X.3.c.02   repaired
X.8.b.75 - 90   repaired
X.3.b.11 - 2   T heads dug and wiring done.

1 Company Sussex also assisted 145th Bde: no details of work to hand.

New Trenches

From X.3.c.0.6½ - for 200 yards W. dug 2' deep.
X.3.c.0.6½ - for 100 yards S.E. dug 1'-6"
X.3.c.93 - X.3.d.28   trench 3ft deep dug.
X.3.d.63 - X.3.d.97   trench started (no details)

Infantry Track.

W.14.a.49 to W.16.b.68 finished.

General.

Work was much delayed owing to heavy shelling and M.G. fire, there being several casualties. The strong point ordered to be constructed at X.3.a. and c 39 - 40 - 50 could not be constructed as the locality was not in our possession.

A.O. Walker
Major R.E.
for C.R.E. 48th Div.

6-30 a.m.
24-7-16.

48th DIVISION.

SUMMARY OF ENGINEER WORK FOR 24 HOURS ENDING 3 a.m. - 23.7.16.

1. **DEFENCE LINE.**   150 yards wired from X.9.c.4.6. towards 82. 2 M.G. emplacements completed, one at X.9.c.4.6. covering road and one 15 yards West of X.9.c.3.2. S.b.9.0. - S.b.3.4. Trench deepened and cleaned.

2. **STRONG POINT.**   LA BOISSELLE KEEP. - 2 M.G. emplacements in hand at N.E. and S.E. corners.

3. **INFANTRY TRACK**   from BOUZINCOURT to AVELUY marked with white topped pickets and bridged for Infantry.

4. **WATER SUPPLY.**   2 wells at LA BOISSELLE under repair: R.A.M.C. state that water from these is drinkable if chlorinated.

6.28 a.m. 23.7.16.

Major R.E.
for C.R.E. 48th Div.

48th DIVISION.

SUMMARY OF ENGINEER WORK FOR 24 HOURS ENDING 3-0 a.m. 22-7-16.

NEW ASSAULT TRENCHES.   L. Sector.   ~~Report not received.~~ *Not dug on account of operations*

                 R. Sector.   X.3.d.05.45 - 35.40 for 150 yards, average section 2½' deep, 2' wide.

                               X.3.d35.40 - X.3.d.63.27 for 120 yards average section 2¼' x 2'

OLD TRENCHES.

11 - 71. Cleared where damaged by shells and several new firebays made.

91 - 85. Good communication trench cleared.

26 - 47. Improved and work put in on bombing stops at 26 and 27.

OVILLERS VILLAGE KEEP.

450 yards wire erected on N. and E. fronts. Trenches cleared on N. side of road and 1 M.G. emplacement made.

ROAD.

(1) AVELUY to LA BOISSELLE - 270 yards of track cleared.

(2) Through OVILLERS - improved.

GENERAL.

Work was impeded by shelling and casualties and by many men having to wear gas masks while working.

6-30 a.m.
22-7-16.

Major R.E.
for C.R.E. 48th Div.

SUMMARY OF ENGINEER WORK CARRIED OUT DURING NIGHT 20/21st
JULY 1916.

3 a.m. report,

* *

1. SUPPORT TRENCH.   11 - 59 - Two new firebays constructed and damages by shelling repaired.

2.   do.   26 - 47 - 120 yards cleared.

2. COMMUNICATION TRENCH.   44 - 47. 300 yards cleaned.

4. OVILLERS KEEP.   67 - 18 - 12. Trench cleared and materials carried to site.

5. ROAD   Through OVILLERS made fit for vehicular traffic up to Church and cleared up to ~~xxxxxxxxxxxxxxxxxxxx~~. S.b.4.4. Can be made good up to S.b.7.8. in four hours.

6. GENERAL.   (a) Work was interfered with by operations.
    (b) No further summary will be issued at noon today.

6.25 p.m. 21.7.16.

A.S. Walker
Major R.E.
for C.R.E. 48th Div

48th DIVISION.

SUMMARY OF ENGINEER WORK CARRIED OUT DURING 24 HOURS ENDING NOON, 20th JULY 1916.

ITEM No.		
1.	DOBBIN STREET (Westland to 99)	completed but latter has since been blown in at point where it meets German front line.
2.	RIVINGTON tunnel appraoch	
3.	05 - 99 (Old German front line)	100 yards cleared and 2 barricades removed.
4.	11 - 59. Support line with 5 firebays completed.	
5.	59 - 61. 70 yards cleared out.	
6.	85 - 88 - 92 – 145 yards trench completed. About 20 yards still remain to make trench passable by day.	
7.	02 - 26. Trench made, also loopholed traverse at 02	
8.	X.2.d.44 - X.3.c.02 - fire position with M.G. emplacement constructed. The trench 44 - 02 - 51 - 93 - 31 - 66 is now passable throughout.	
9.	Trench from X.9.b.65 N.W., cleaned and deepened for 125 yards.	
10. STRONG POINT.	At point 73 (tramway junction) constructed.	
11. TRENCH FOR CORPS SIGNALS.	X.9.a.66 - X.9.c.46. Trench 3' deep dug. X.9.c.46 - X.8.d.70. gap. X.8.d.70 - X.14.a.95. Trench 1' deep dug.	
12. ROAD.	Through OVILLERS - width increased to 15ft and now fit for traffic up to 8.b.23 beyond the church except at two points. ~~Bridg~~ Bridges delivered and should be in position by 2-0 p.m. to-day. Road has been rather badly shelled since work stopped.	
13. WELLS	Two more discovered in OVILLERS and being opened up and sample of water being obtained. Sample of water from well at 95 sent to A.D.M.S.	

The items in the above appeared in the 3-0 a.m. report with the exception of item 13. Additional notes have been made to items 2, 6, 8, and 12.

Major R.E.
for C.R.E. 48th Div

3-30 p.m.
20-7-16.

48th DIVISION.

SUMMARY OF ENGINEER WORK CARRIED OUT DURING 24 HOURS.
ENDING NOON 19-7-16.

TRENCHES. X.2.c.11 to within 50 yards of X.3.a.59 prepared for fire.

RIVINGTON TUNNEL approach and WESTLAND trench across No Man's Land deepened and widened.

X.3.a.52 - 46, cleared as communication trench

X.3.a.95 - 88, (100 yds) ditto.   ditto.

X.2.d.4.4. - X.3.c.0.2. Being worked on.

(Condition :- 2.d.4.4. - 2.d.3.2. Only 2ft deep.
 2.d.3.2. - 3.c.0.2. 3½' deep and passable by day.)

X.9.b.9.8. -X.3.d.5½.2½. (250 yards)) New trenches got out to
X.3.d.3.1. -X.3.d.5½.2½. (100 ")) a depth of 3ft. and
X.9.b.4.8. -X.3.d.7.0.   ) breadth 2½ ft.

ROAD THROUGH OVILLERS. Cleared and levelled from point X.3.c.1.5. to the Church, (95% completed).

WELL. At about 8.b.9.6. under repair.

BOMB STOPS. Constructed 200 yards along N.E. trench from 3.c.0.2. to 79, also near 2.d.4.4.

1-0 p.m.
19-7-16.

Major R.E.
for C R.E. 48th Div.

48th DIVISION

SUMMARY OF R.E. WORK CARRIED OUT DURING NIGHT
18/19th JULY 1916.

3 a.m. report.

* * * * * * * * * * * * * * * * * * *

TRENCHES. X.9.b.9.8. - X.3.d.5½.2½. (250 yds.)) New trenches got out
X.3.d.3.1. - X.3.d.5½.2½. (100 yds.)) to a depth of 3 ft.
X.9.b.4.8. - X.3.d.7.0.) and breadth 2½ ft.

X.2.c.1.1. - X.2.c.6.1. (300 yds.) Cleared and fire bays started.

RIVINGTON TUNNEL approach and WESTLAND trench across No Man's Land deepened and widened.

X.2.d.4.4. - X.3.c.0.2.   Being worked on.

(Condition :- 2.d.4.4. - 2.d.8.2. Only 2 ft. deep.
2.d.8.2. - 3.c.0.2. 3½' deep and passable by day.

Road through OVILLERS. Cleared and levelled from point X.3.c.1.5. to the Church (95% completed).

WELL at about 8.b.9.6. under repair.

* * * * * * * * * * * * * * *

BOMB STOPS. Constructed 200 yards along N.E. trench from 3.c.0.2. to 79, also near 2.d.4.4.

[signature]
Major R.E.
for C R.E. 48th Div

48th DIVISION.

SUMMARY OF ENGINEER WORK CARRIED OUT DURING 24 HOURS ENDING NOON 18-7-16.

COMMUNICATIONS.

WESTLAND trench communication to German front line (point X.7.b.99) excavated to 3' depth (distance 250 yards including zig-zags)

RIVINGTON tunnel broken through and continued to German front line.

X. 14.a.67 - 59 - 98 up to X.8.d.24 communication trench cleared
X.8.b.7.5. - X.8.b.90   "   "   "
X.9.c.46   - X.8.b.90   "   "   "
X.9.b.77   - X.9.c.64   "   "   "
X.14.a.94 - X.14.c.46   "   "   "

FRONT LINE.

Trench dug and firebays cut along our new line X.2.d.44, X.2.d.02, X.2.c.92 and support line behind it.

STRONG POINT.

LA BOISSELLE M.G. emplacements and dug-outs in course of construction on N.W. and N.E. faces.

Headquarters "G",
    48th Division.

            For your information.

Major R.E.
for C.R.E. 48th Div.

18-7-16.

48th Divisional Engineers

C. R. E.

48th DIVISION

AUGUST 1 9 1 6

Report on Engineer Work attached.

Army Form C. 2118.

WAR DIARY
or
INTELLIGENCE SUMMARY.
(Erase heading not required.)

Instructions regarding War Diaries and Intelligence Summaries are contained in F. S. Regs., Part II. and the Staff Manual respectively. Title pages will be prepared in manuscript.

Place	Date 1916	Hour	Summary of Events and Information	Remarks and references to Appendices
DOMQUEUR	AUG. 1.		At DOMQUEUR	
	2.		At DOMQUEUR	
	3.		Companies moved to l'ETOILE for Pontooning.	
	4.		Field Companies and 5th R.Sussex Pioneers erected Pontoon	
	5.		and service trestle bridges, returning on evening of 5th Aug. 1916.	
	6.		At DOMQUEUR.	
	7.		At DOMQUEUR.	
	8.		At DOMQUEUR. Companies moved to LEALVILLERS.	
BEAUVAL.	9.		R.E. Headquarters moved to BEAUVAL. Companies moved to AUTHIEULE.	
	10.		Companies moved to ACHEUX.	
	11.		At BEAUVAL.	
	12.		At BEAUVAL.	
BOUZINCOURT.	13.		R.E. Headquarters moved to BOUZINCOURT. Companies moved to AVELUY.	
	14. to 27.		At BOUZINCOURT, see attached Summary.	
BERTRANCOURT	28.		R.E. Headquarters moved to BERTRANCOURT.	

1577 Wt.W10791/1773 500,000 1/15 D. D. & L. A.D.S.S./Forms/C. 2118.

Army Form C. 2118.

WAR DIARY
or
INTELLIGENCE SUMMARY.
(Erase heading not required.)

Instructions regarding War Diaries and Intelligence Summaries are contained in F. S. Regs., Part II. and the Staff Manual respectively. Title pages will be prepared in manuscript.

Place	Date 1916 AUG.	Hour	Summary of Events and Information	Remarks and references to Appendices
BERTRANCOURT	28		1st S.M.Field Coy. R.E. moved to BUS.	
			2nd S.M.Field Coy. R.E. moved to AUTHIE.	
	29/31		2/1st S.M.Field Coy. R.E. moved to MAILLY - MAILLET.	
			At BERTRANCOURT.	

[signature]
Major R.E.
for **C.R.E.** 48th Div.

Report on Engineer work carried out by the 48th Division
in connection with active operations in front of AVELUY
between 13th and 23rd August 1916.
* *

13.8.16.   C.R.E. took over during the day from C.R.E., 12th Division;
           Hd. Qrs. at BOUZINCOURT.

           Three Field Companies arrived on same day from ACHEUX and
           bivouacked near AVELUY, two sections each of 1st and 2nd
           Field Companies being sent forward to dugouts at RIBBLE
           STREET.   One section of 3rd Field Company was retained at
           BOUZINCOURT to look after stores, workshops and water supply

           R.E. officers were sent out the same day to report on
           communication trenches, water supply, tramways, etc.

           The Pioneers had arrived four days previously and had been
           working under the 12th Division.

           The R.E. and Pioneers of the 12th Division remained on
           until the 17th August working under the 48th Division.

           At night the R.E. and Pioneers worked on clearing communi-
           cation trenches and on preparing and continuing tramway
           line.

14.8.16.   Work was done during night of 14/15 August as follows:-

           Strong points were made or improved as near the Infantry as
           circumstances would permit, i.e. at X.2.c.8.7. - X.2.d.2.3.-
           X.3.c.7.9. - X.3.b.5.4. - X.3.a.0.4. - R.32.d.9.0.(bomb stop
           only).

           A good deal of work was put in on clearing communication
           trenches which were continually being damaged by heavy
           shelling.

           On this night the Germans made a ~~successful~~ counter attack
           on SKYLINE trench and work in our Right Sector was in
           consequence impeded by shelling.

           The construction of the tramway line was proceeded with
           formation being made for 130 yards and 200 yards of track
           being collected.

           12th Divisional R.E. and Pioneers worked at OVILLERS
           defences and dugouts, Brigade Hd. Qrs. DONNET and USNA,
           trenchboarding 2nd Avenue and revetting 3rd Street North
           of OVILLERS.

15.8.16.   1st (ZERO AVENUE) transferred to Anzac Division.

           SKYLINE trench was re-occupied during the night.

           A new communication trench between SKYLINE and RATION
           trenches from R.33.c.9.2. to R.33.c.6.9. was started; the
           Southern portion of it was dug to a depth of 3½ ft. for a
           length of 290 yards.

           RATION trench, which suffered badly from shelling during
           these operations, was thoroughly repaired
                                                    MOY AVENUE

- 2 -

15.8.16. MOY AVENUE, which had also been blown in between X.3.c.0.2. and X.8.b.7.8., was deepened and improved.

Communication trenches in the Left Sector also received attention.

The strong points started on the previous day were repaired.

Tramway construction proceeded.

A new Brigade Hd. Qrs. at GLOUCESTER POST was improved and made suitable for occupation.

The 12th Division R.E. and Pioneers continued work as on previous night.

16.8.16. The 12th Division R.E. and Pioneers handed over work in hand to 48th Division R.E. and Pioneers.

During the night an attempt to work on communication trenches between RATION trench and SKYLINE trench was abandoned owing to heavy shelling. Other communication trenches however received attention.

Strong points continued to be improved and repaired. A new strong point was constructed on SKYLINE trench at R.33.c.1.4.

The tramway was completed as far as X.3.c.8.1.

OVILLERS KEEP was further improved.

17.8.16. A further attempt was made to open up communication trenches between RATION and SKYLINE trenches; this attempt was successful three trenches being got through during the night.

Communication trenches in the Left Sector also received attention.

Strong points at R.33.c.1.4. and X.3.a.2.6. were worked upon.

The tramway line was completed up to X.3.c.7.9.

Brigade Hd. Qrs. at GLOUCESTER POST were completed.

Work continued on OVILLERS KEEP.

18.8.16. On the afternoon of the 18th a successful attack was made at 5-0 p.m. by the 143rd Bde. on the left sector. Two Forward Observing R.E. Officers, each with 6 men, were sent forward following the attack. These parties were for the purpose of erecting bombstops and clearing mouths of dugouts.

Two sections of R.E., who had been in readiness under cover N. of OVILLERS, acting under instructions from the Forward Observing Officers, proceeded at 7-30 p.m. for the construction of strong points in the captured trenches. They were relieved at 2-0 a.m. by a 2nd relief.

The Pioneers were similarly kept ready for the purpose of clearing communications to the front. Acting on instructions from their own reconnoitring Officers they proceeded at 7-0 p.m. to clear 1st, 2nd, 3rd & 4th Streets.

As the occupation of SKYLINE TRENCH during daylight was, on account of its exposed position, liable to heavy casualties, a new trench in rear of the skyline, X.2.b.99 to R.33.c.93 (BRIMSTONE TRENCH) was started.

RATION trench was consolidated and strong points put in.

Work continued on OVILLERS KEEP.

- 3 -

19.8.16.   BRIMSTONE trench was completed as a fire trench and communication trenches between SKYLINE and RATION trenches were cleaned out.

Work on OVILLERS defences was continued.

Strong points were constructed at the following places:-

X.2.a.22 - X.2.a.96 - X.2.a.80 - X.2.b.03 - X.2.b.20 - X.2.b.62 - X.2.b.86.

20.8.16.   BRIMSTONE trench was further improved, traverses being made and 200 yards of wire fence was erected in front of it.

Work on strong points started on previous night was continued.
Eleven deep dugouts were started.
Communication trenches were worked upon.

Work on OVILLERS KEEP was continued.

21.8.16.   On the afternoon of this day a successful attack was made on the Left Sector. *The same arrangements were made as on the 18th Inst. as regards Forward Observing Officer & parties of R.E. & Pioneers*
Work on trenches in R.33.c. was continued.

Communication trenches from AINTREE Street to X.1.b.19 and from X.1.b.90 - X.2.a.22 across No Man's Land were started.

Strong point was made at X.1.b.19.

1st Street was cleared up to R.31.d.81.

Work continued on OVILLERS KEEP and on deep dugouts.

22.8.16.   Work on BRIMSTONE Avenue continued.

Communication trenches started on previous night across No Man's Land were deepened and communication trench X.1.b.19 to R.31.d.30 was cleared.

Work on deep dugouts and OVILLERS defences continued.

23.8.16.   A large strong point on SKYLINE trench at R.33.c.46 was started.

Strong point R.33.c.14 was worked upon.

Communication trenches between SKYLINE and RATION trenches and also Left Sector were cleared.

Work on deep dugouts and OVILLERS defences continued.

The strong points

- 4 -

24.8.16.
The strong points on SKYLINE trench were further improved.
Work on communication trenches was put in.
R.E. dumps were started at X.3.a.15 and X.2.a.22.
Work on deep dugouts and OVILLERS defences continued.

26ᵗʰ

25.8.16.
Strong point R.33.c.14 completed.
Trench X.2.b.59 - X.2.b.43 completed and fire-bayed.
Communication trenches were worked upon and work continued on deep dugouts.

25ᵗʰ

26.8.16.
106th Field Co.R.E. of the 25th Division arrived at AVELUY.
Strong points were made in SULPHUR AVENUE.
A new fire trench was constructed from X.3.a.31 to X.2.b.30.
The Divisional main line which ran from X.3.b.89 along SULPHUR AVENUE to X.3.a.31 thence to X.2.b.30 - X.2.d.47 - 28 - X.2.c.66 - 57 - was consolidated throughout and prepared for defence.
Trench R.32.d.91 to X.2.b.59 was prepared as a fire trench.
Work on deep dugouts was continued.

26ᵗʰ

27.8.16.

Attack started 7 p.m. F.O.O. with attack sent for R.E. and Pioneers who were in readiness at about 9-0 p.m.

105ᵗ Fd. Coy R.E. of the 25ᵗʰ Division arrived at AVELUY.
An attack by both Brigades was made late in the evening. A Section of R.E. and half a Company of Pioneers were sent to follow each Brigade in its attack. On the right these parties dug a new trench from X.2.b.38 to R.32.d.30. On the left they consolidated from the latter point through 91 - 79 - 31 - X.2.a.19.

Communication trenches were kept cleared, the Divisional main line was further consolidated and work on dugouts was continued.

28.8.16.
The Division handed over to the 25th Division.

R.E. Hd.Qrs. moved to BERTRANCOURT.
1st Field Co.R.E. moved to BUS.
2nd Field Co. R.E. moved to AUTHIE.
3rd Field Co. R.E. moved to MAILLY MAILLET.

28ᵗʰ

＊＊＊＊＊＊＊＊＊＊＊＊＊＊＊＊＊＊＊＊＊＊＊＊

29.8.16.

Major R.E.
For C.R.E., 48th Division.

48th. DIVISIONAL ENGINEERS

C. R. E.

48th. DIVISION

SEPTEMBER 1916.

R.E. HEAD QUARTERS
No. 848/R.E.
30 SEP 1916
48th DIVISION.

CONFIDENTIAL.

WAR DIARY

of

48th (South Midland) Divisional Engineers.

From 1st September 1916......to,,,,,,30th September 1916.

(Volume 19.)

Army Form C. 2118.

WAR DIARY
or
INTELLIGENCE SUMMARY.
(Erase heading not required.)

Instructions regarding War Diaries and Intelligence Summaries are contained in F. S. Regs., Part II. and the Staff Manual respectively. Title pages will be prepared in manuscript.

Place	Date	Hour	Summary of Events and Information	Remarks and references to Appendices
BERTRANCOURT.	1916. Sept. 1.		At BERTRANCOURT.	
	2.		do.	
BEAUVAL.	3.		R.E. Hd. Qrs. moved to BEAUVAL.	
	4/9.		At BEAUVAL.	
	10.		2/1st S.M. Field Co. R.E. moved from MAILLY MAILLET to WARNIMONT WOOD.	
	11.		1/1st, 1/2nd and 2/1st S.M. Field Cos. moved to LONGUEVILLETTE.	
HEM.	13.		R.E. Hd. Qrs. and 3 Field Cos. moved to HEM.	
	18.		R.E. Hd. Qrs. and 2/1st S.M. Field Co. R.E. moved to MEZEROLLES.	
			1/1st S.M. Field Co. R.E. moved to OCCOCHES.	
			1/2nd S.M. Field Co. R.E. moved to OUTREBOIS.	
BERNAVILLE.	24.		R.E. Hd. Qrs. and 1/2nd and 2/1st S.M. Field Cos. moved to BERNAVILLE.	
			1/1st S.M. Field Co. R.E. moved to CANDAS.	
	29.		1/1st S.M. Field Co. R.E. moved to SOMBORIN.	
			1/2nd S.M. Field Co. R.E. moved to CAUMESNIL.	
			2/1st S.M. Field Co. R.E. moved to SUS ST. LEGER.	
HENU.	30.		R.E. Hd. Qrs. moved to HENU.	
			Month spent generally in rest and in training,	

Major R.E.
for C.R.E. 48th Div

R.E. HEAD QUARTERS
No............
31 OCT 1916
48th. DIVISION.

CONFIDENTIAL.

WAR DIARY

of

48th (South Midland) Divisional Engineers.

From 1st October 1916......to.....31st October 1916.

(Volume 20.)

Army Form C. 2118.

WAR DIARY
or
INTELLIGENCE SUMMARY.
(Erase heading not required.)

Instructions regarding War Diaries and Intelligence Summaries are contained in F. S. Regs., Part II. and the Staff Manual respectively. Title pages will be prepared in manuscript.

Place	Date	Hour	Summary of Events and Information	Remarks and references to Appendices
HENU.	1916. Oct. 1.		At HENU.	
	1.		1/1st S.M. Field Co. R.E. moved to GAUDIEMPRE.	
			2/1st S.M. Field Co. R.E. moved to HALLOY.	
			48th Division took over "W" Sector from 49th Division.	
	2.		1/2nd S.M. Field Co. R.E. moved to SAILLY and HEBUTERNE.	
			48th Division took over "Y" Sector from 49th Division.	
	3.		2/1st S.M. Field Co. R.E. moved to GRENAS.	
	4.		1/1st S.M. Field Co. R.E. moved to LA HALE FARM.	
			1/2nd S.M. Field Co. R.E. moved to HENU.	
			2/1st S.M. Field Co. R.E. Hd. Qrs. and 2 Sections moved to SOUASTRE, and 2 Sections to FONQUEVILLERS.	
	5/20.		See attached reports on work.	
	20.		1/1st S.M. Field Co. R.E. moved to WARLINGCOURT.	
	21.		R.E. Hd. Qrs. moved to DOULLENS.	
			1/2nd and 2/1st Field Cos. R.E. moved to WARLINGCOURT.	
	22.		1/1st S.M. Field Co. R.E. moved to BEAUVAL.	
	23.		R.E. Hd. Qrs. moved to BAIZIEUX.	
			1/1st S.M. Field Co. R.E. moved to TALMAS.	
	24.		1/1st S.M. Field Co. R.E. moved to LAHOUSSOYE.	
	25.		1/1st S.M. Field Co. R.E. moved to ALBERT.	
			1/2nd S.M. Field Co. R.E. moved to FRANVILLERS.	
			2/1st S.M. Field Co. R.E. moved to BRESLE.	

Army Form C. 2118.

WAR DIARY
or
INTELLIGENCE SUMMARY.
(Erase heading not required.)

Instructions regarding War Diaries and Intelligence Summaries are contained in F. S. Regs., Part II. and the Staff Manual respectively. Title pages will be prepared in manuscript.

Place	Date	Hour	Summary of Events and Information	Remarks and references to Appendices
	1916. Oct. 26.		1/ 2nd S.M. Field Co. R.E. moved to MAMETZ WOOD. 2/1st S.M. Field Co. R.E. moved to MAMETZ WOOD.	
	27.			
	28.		1/1st S.M. Field Co. R.E. moved to near CONTALMAISON (X.17.a.9.4.)	
	29.			
	30.			
	31.		R.E. Hd. Qrs. moved to MILLENCOURT.	

[signature]
Major R.E.
for C.R.E. 48th Div

48th DIVISION.

Report on R.E. work for 24 hours ending 6 a.m. 4.10.16.

RIGHT SECTOR. (1. Bttn. 17th Div. Pioneers, 1.Company 33rd Div. Pioneers, 1. Company 48th Div. R.E.)

Communication Trenches.

Welcome Street.) Whiskey Street.) Woman Street (R to C))	Cleaned and repaired.
Wurzel Street.	Cleaned, repaired and 70 yards trench boards laid.
Yankee Street.	Revetted.

Assemble and Fire Trenches.

C (Woman to Wood)	Deepened but requires trench boarding, revetting & draining.
D (Woman to Wood)	ditto.
R (Woman to Wood)	Sandbags carried and emptied.

Deep dugouts.

No. 1. between Yankee Street and Jellow Street.	Gallery connected through and dugout commenced.
No. 2. (in R.between Whiskey and Woman)	N.gallery 4ft.in S. " 12ft.in.
No. 3. (in R.between Wood and Woman)	N.gallery 6ft.in S. " 3ft.in

LEFT SECTOR. (5th Royal Sussex Pioneers.)

Communication Trenches.

Yellow Street.	Cleaned and revetted.
Young.	Revetted and repaired.
Yussif.	Drained and trenchboards relaid.
Nab.	Revetted and 150 yards trenchboards laid.

Assembly trenches.

C.	Deepened and cleaned.
D.	do.

GENERAL. Rain was continuous throughout the day and the state of the trenches was very bad in consequence.

Major R.E.
For C.R.E., 48th Division.

1 p.m.
4.10.16.

O/C

48th DIVISION.

Report on R.E. work for 24 hours ending 6 a.m., 5-10-16.
****

RIGHT SECTOR.   (1.Battn. 17th Div. Pioneers, 2 Companies 5th Sussex Pioneers 1.Field Coy. R.E.)

SOUASTRE FORK	Repair of road.	Work completed.
D.line (YIDDISH to GOMMECOURT Road)	Trench repairs.	
R. line.(WOOD ST. to WOMAN.)	ditto.	
NAB.	Revetting, sumps and trenchboarding.	
YOUNG STREET.	Revetting, sandbagging, trenchboarding.	
D. line. (Yiddish to YOUNG.)	Deepening and cleaning. Nearly completed.	
WOMAN ST. (between C. and B. line)	Sandbagging and cleaning.	
WOOD ST.	Sump.	
WURZEL ST.	Trenchboarding and cleaning.	
~~WHISKEY ST.~~ WELCOME ST.	Cleaning, sumping, deepening.	
WHISKEY ST.	Sandbagging, cleaning.	
YANKEE ST.) YIDDISH ST.) WOMAN ST.) WHISKEY ST.)	T.M. emplacements.)Sandbagging. do.)Revetting. Finished. do.)Cleaning. do.)etc.	

HEBUTERNE.   (1 Field Coy. R.E.)

	C. and D. trenches. firing line.	Improving cleaning and revetting.
SAILLY.	Repairing 3 unsafe buildings.	Work completed.

2 Companies Middlesex Pioneers
CROSS ST.
K10 c 28 to K10 c 53   Deepening throughout 18"
                      J.K. Sainsbury
K10 c 5.3   do   Lt RE
to K.16 a 9.8½   for CRE 48

48th Division.

Report on R.E. work for 24 hours ending 6 a.m. 6.10.16.

17th Div. Area. Communication trenches.

WELCOME STREET.	110 yards trenchboarded, 300 yards deepened, and sandbags cleared.
WHISKEY STREET.	Repairs and revetting.
WOMAN STREET.	New portion: revetting and screening. Old portion: 12 revetting frames and 10 trenchboards put in.
WURZEL STREET. (D.to B.)	200 yards trenchboards laid, clearing and widening.

TRENCH MORTAR EMPLACEMENTS.

One Company Pioneers employed on 4 emplacements, sandbagging, revetting, etc.

48th Div. Area.

RIGHT SECTOR.

Communication trenches.

YORK ST. and YOUNG ST.	One Company Pioneers cleaning and draining.

Communications.

From BLUFF DUMP towards CAT MILL — 350 yards trenchboarded
Road past CAT MILL. — (1.Coy. Pioneers) cleaned.

LEFT SECTOR.

Communication trenches.

6th AVENUE.	200 yards cleaned.
KELLERMAN.	200 yards cleaned.
YUSSIF.	160 yards cleaned.
YUZ.	130 yards cleaned.
THORPE ST.(CALVAIRE to MOUSETRAP)	20 yards widened & revetted
MILL STREET.	Cleaned and trenchboarded, throughout except for 100 yards.
VALLEY AVENUE.	Cleaned throughout.

O.P'.s. Div. O.P. site cleared and work started.

Brigade O.P. in THORPE STREET. cleared and work started.

R.E. Dump.   at K.3.d.32: Stores collected.

Tramline.   K.1.d.90 to THORPE STREET: cleared throughout,
             and 4 trollies collected and repaired.

WATER TANK   at entrance to THORPE STREET raised & protected.

                                          Major R.E.
                                For C.R.E., 48th Division.

1 p.m.
6.10.16.

48th DIVISION.

Report on R.E. work for 24 hours ending 6 a.m. 7.10.16.

17th Div. Area. No report received except from 18th Middlesex Pioneers (3rd ~~Div~~) who cleared and trenchboarded CROSS STREET as under:-

    K.10.c.2.8. - K.10.c.53.   50 boards laid.

    K.10.c.53 - K.16.a.9.3½.   Trench completed except for 30 yards.

48th Div. Area.

RIGHT SECTOR.

Assembly Trenches.

D. line right of GOMMECOURT ROAD. Cleaning and draining.

Communication Trenches.

YOUNG.)   Repaired; permanent maintenance gang of
YORK.)
YIDDISH.) Pioneers will now be put on these.
YELLOW.)

Track BLUFF DUMP to CAT MILL.   Trenchboards laid but not fastened.

Advanced Div. Hd. Qrs.   Trenches for communications cleared and plans completed.

LEFT SECTOR.

Communication Trenches.

KELLERMAN.	40 yards boarded, 60 yards cleaned.
6th AVENUE.	40 " " 300 " "
YUSSIF.	All trenchboards, 120 " " repaired.
YUZ.	20 yards drained and boarded.
EBLE STREET.	130 yards cleaned, boards repaired & relaid.
THORPE STREET.	200 yards " " " " "

MOUSE TRAP POST switch.   All wire entanglement removed and barricade at Mouse Trap end cut through.

O.Ps. Div.   Excavation finished and one side revetted.
      Bde.   Framework erected and sides revetted.

TRAMLINE.   K.1.d.90 to THORPE STREET cleaned and in working order throughout.

                                              Major R.E.
12.15 p.m. 7.10.16.   For C.R.E., 48th Div.

DAILY WORK REPORT.

For 24 hours ending 6 a.m. 9-10-16.

Nature of Work.	Location of work.	Number of Infantry employed (if any)	Progress of work.	REMARKS.
RIGHT SECTOR.				**RIGHT SECTOR.**
ASSEMBLY TRENCHES.				
Cleaning & Sumping.	B.Line.		1-Company for one day still needed.	
	D.Line,Rt.		1-Platoon day still needed.	
COMMUNICATION TRENCHES.				
MAINTENANCE	Y-trenches & NAP.		Proceeding.	5th Sussex permanent starts on NAP on 9th.
Straightening	NAP-YOUNG		Digging complete- trenchboarding not yet finished.	
O.P.				
Constructed	YELLOW-R		Proceeding	
Advanced H.Q.				
Boarding dugouts) Sandbagging.) Horse shelter) Mending dugouts.)	LA HAIE.			
DUMPS FORWARD.				
Digging.	Top of YOUNG. Top of YELLOW.		Nearly completed.	
LEFT SECTOR.				**LEFT SECTOR.**
ASSEMBLY TRENCHES.				
Collecting & erecting trench ladders.	2nd Line		125 ladders placed in position.	70 more collected. Approach trench to be cleaned
COMMUNICATION TRENCHES.				
Cleaning, draining, & boarding.	NAP ST.		Cleaned and drained	About 250 yds. to be boarded.
" "	KELLERMAN		Cleaned & drained, 150 yds. boarded.	About 250 yds. to be boarded.
" "	6th STREET		Cleaned, drained & boarded throughout.	40 Inf. employed as carrying party.
" "	Approach trench to NEW TUNNEL.		100 yds. cleaned & boarded.	
Cleaning & draining	N. of SOUASTRE FONQUEVILLERS Road.		75 yds. pumped out & cleaned.	1 Platoon Pioneers 2 days to complete.
O.P's				
Div. O.P.	Nr. M.G.3		Completed	
Bde. O.P.	THORPE ST.		Completed	
Signals O.P.	do.		Excavation complete, bed plates & uprights erected, sides revetted, frames made in shop.	1 day to complete No R.A. working party turned up.
DUGOUTS.				
Dugout for 242 Bde.	Nr. Bde.O.P.		Frames made in shop.	No. R.A. working party turned up.
3 Signal Shelters.	Front line. Support Line ADDIS ST.		Excavations done & frames made in shop.	1 day to complete.
SCREENS.	SOUASTRE- FONQUEVILLERS Rd.		Grass screens being prepared in shop.	5 days to complete

DAILY WORK REPORT.

For 24 hours ending 6 a.m. 8-10-16.

RIGHT SECTOR.

Work Number.	Nature of Work.	Location of Work.	Number of Infantry employed (if any)	Progress of Work.	REMARKS.
Assembly trenches.	Cleaning & Deepening	B-line	1½ Coys Pioneers.	Behind hand by ½ a day	Large number of buried Sandbags and trenchboards made excavations very slow
"	Cleaning, deepening & Draining.	D-line Right.	Pioneers	3 Sumps made and revetting where required.	Much wire work needed, probably ½ Coy. 1 night and day.
Commn. trenches.	Shortening & improving trench.	NAP to YOUNG	80 Bucks.	Begun at all points.	Another days work for section R.E. and 2 platoons Pioneers wanted, ordered for 8th. 100 Infantry were promised only 80 appeared and they only worked 2½ hours
"	Cleaning	SOLFERINO	16 Pioneers	- - - - - - - - - - - - - - -	Another similar party required
"	"	Y trenches	36 "	- - - - - - - - - - - - - - -	Maintenance Gangs.
"	Laying Trenchboards	BLUFF - CAT	-	Another Section-day required.	
O.P.	Site selected & Materials collected.	Junct. of YELLOW & R.	Nil.	-	
DUMPS.	Formation.	BLUFF & CAT MILL	120 Bucks.	Slow	Only 120 men arrived - 200 at least expected for carrying party.
"	Digging	Off YOUNG near top	-	20ˣ length 8'wide x 5'deep	Length of Assembly trench being widened to 8' for 25ˣ.
Adv.H.Q.	Sentry Post Trenches Sand bagging	SOUASTRE Rd LA HAIE "	- -	Trenches finished	Should have some trenchboards.

LEFT SECTOR.

Work Number.	Nature of Work.	Location of Work.	Number of Infantry employed	Progress of Work.	REMARKS.
1.	Cleaning, draining, & boarding.	KELLERMAN		The whole has been cleaned & drained. 100 yds trenchboards laid.	
2.	ditto.	6th STREET		2 drains widened & deepened 336 yds. of trenchboard laid.	Complete.
3.	Upkeep	THORPE ST.		Damaged trench boards for a distance of 650 yds.	Except for daily upkeep THORPE ST. is finished.
4.	Cleaning, draining, & boarding.	NAP ST. from KELLERMAN to THORPE ST.		Cleaned throughout.	A few sumps still to be pumped out, about 200 yds of trenchboards required to complete.
5.	Div'l O.P.	Near M.G.3.		1 Frame fitted, 2 others prepared & ready to fit.	1 days work to complete.
6.	Bde. O.P.	THORPE ST.		Girders fixed on roof & ready for concrete. Inside fittings complete	Will be finished by 6 a.m. 9-10-16.
7.	Signals.O.P.	ditto.		Excavation complete & framework made, ready for erection.	2 days to complete.
8.	Dugout for 242 Bde.	Nr.Bde.O.P.		Excavation nearly complete. Frames made.	4 days to complete.
9.	Sundry R.E.work			Shelter made for trench disinfector at SOUASTRE. Horse driven pump at SOUASTRE being repaired. etc, etc.,	

R.E. HEAD QUARTERS
No.
8 OCT 1916
48th DIVISION.

Major R.E.
for C.R.E. 48th Div

DAILY WORK REPORT.

For 24 hours ending 6 a.m. 10-10-16.

Stamp: 10 OCT 1916 48th. DIVISION.

Nature of Work.	Location of Work.	Progress of work.	REMARKS.
RIGHT SECTOR.			**RIGHT SECTOR.**
ASSEMBLY TRENCHES.			
Cleaning, deepening & trenchboarding.	B.Line YANKEE-YIDDISH.		Completed YANKEE-YIDDISH.
" "	YIDDISH to Z. hedge		
" "	D.Line YANKEE to YIDDISH		1 Platoon day still required.
" "	YIDDISH-YUSSUF		1 more nights work needed still.
Laying Trenchboards	LA HAIE-BLUFF		Two days work still required.
COMMUNICATION TRENCHES.			
Maintenance.	YELLOW YIDDISH YOUNG NAP	S	Party for NAP, of 1 N.C.O. & 5 men billetted at CAT MILL. 700 Trenchboards still reqd. for YIDDISH.
Straightening & Trenchboarding	NAP-SOLFERINO		Requires 1 Platoon day to complete
O's			
Excavating and constructing overhead cover.	Corner of YELLOW & R.		Should be completed by night of 11th
D. H.Q.			
Boarding dugouts and making horse shelters	LA HAIE.		
LEFT SECTOR.			**LEFT SECTOR.**
ASSEMBLY TRENCHES.			
Cleaning, draining & boarding	KELLERMAN	Cleaned throughout, 100 trenchboards laid.	1 day to complete.
" " "	Approach trench to New Tunnel (?TUNNEL ST.)	45 yds. Cleaned & drained	Work will be continued by night only.
Cleaning & draining	N. side of SOUASTRE-FONQUEVILLERS Rd.	30 yds. more to complete	1 days work to deepen drains & sumps.
O's.			
Div. O.P. Signal O.P.	Nr. N.G.3 THORPE ST.	Approach trench cleaned All ready to take roof, sides revetted.	Work in O.P. finished. Roof will be put on to-night.
DUGOUTS.			
Dugout for D/242	Nr. Bde. O.P.	Excavation complete, frames all made.	Frames will be carried up to-morrow and fitted during the day.
Signal shelters	Front Line Support Line	Excavation complete & all material for shelter carried to site.	1 day to complete.
TUNNEL.	CALVAIRE to TUNNEL ST.	21' completed	54' to be done. (3 days)
DUMPS.	EBLIE ST. & YUZ.	Stores and Tools dumped.	
TRAMLINE.	FONQUEVILLERS to CRUCIFIX	Repaired up to 6th STREET. Level crossing made.	
SCREEN.	SOUASTRE - FONQUEVILLERS RD.	20 yds. new screen erected 20 " repaired.	
SUNDRY R.E. WORK.		Artillery trench bridge made & erected. 97 sign boards painted, etc., etc.,	

Signed Major R.E.
for C.R.E. 48th Div.

DAILY WORK REPORT.

For 24 hours ending 6 a.m. 11-10-16.

Nature of Work.	Location of Work.	Progress of Work.	REMARKS.
RIGHT SECTOR.			**RIGHT SECTOR.**
ASSEMBLY TRENCHES.			
Cleaning & boarding Placing Trench Ladders	B.line.		
ditto.	C.Line.	In charge of occupying Infantry.	Special report to-night on progress.
ditto.	D.right	Complete except for some trenchboards still awaited	
ditto.	D.left	& ladders not placed.	
FORWARD DUMPS.			
Digging & screening	YELLOW & YOUNG	Complete.	
Filling	YOUNG	Proceeding to-day.	
COMMUNICATION TRENCHES.			
Repairs	All		Permanent repair gangs.
Cleaning & boarding	YIDDISH	Up from KEEP entrance & down from FONQUEVILLERS Rd. parties are working to meet. Work continuing to-day, also cut from GOMMECOURT ROAD to YIDDISH, to straighten it.	
Laying trenchboard track	BLUFF to LA HAIE	Two more days required to straightening it also 440' Trenchboards.	
Deviating rail	K.1.a.14 to J.5.b.97	One more day needed.	
ADVD. HD. QRS.			
Preparing for occupation.	LA HAIE	Horse shelter complete, boarding of dugout proceeding.	
O.Ps.	YELLOW-R.	In progress	
LEFT SECTOR.			**LEFT SECTOR.**
COMMUNICATION TRENCHES.			
Cleaning & boarding	KELLERMAN.	Boarded throughout	Complete.
ditto.	CALVAIRE to MOUSE TRAP.	Cleaned and boarded as far as Miner's tramway.	No more can be done so long as tramway is being used.
Cleaning & draining	N. of FONQUEVILLERS-SOUASTRE Road.	Cleaned and drained throughout	Complete.
Cleaning, draining, and boarding.	TUNNEL ST.	70 yds. cleaned out & deepened.	One night to complete.
O.Ps.			
Div'l O.P. & Signal O.P.		Completed.	
DUGOUTS.			
Dugout for D/242	Nr. Bde. O.P.	Frames carried up	Very little work done. R.A. working party withdrawn owing to shelling.
3 Signal Shelters.	Front line Support line EBLIE ST.	2 completed. Excavations for 3rd done & frames on site	
TUNNEL.	CALVAIRE to TUNNEL ST.	33' in all completed.	
RATION RECESSES.	THORPE ST.	All rations recessed into parapet.	
TRENCH LADDERS.	Assembly trenches	All ladders required stacked in Assembly trenches. Most of them erected.	
TRAMLINE.	6th STREET to TUNNEL ST.	New track laid to MILL ST.	1 night to complete.
SUNDRY R.E. WORK.		Screen on FONQUEVILLERS-SOUASTRE Road thickened. White direction boards painted. Trench bridges made. Bangalore Torpedoes made.	

Major R.E.
for C.R.E. 48th Div.

DAILY WORK REPORT.

For 24 hours ending 6 a.m. 12-10-16.

R.E. HEA[...] No. 9971[...]
12 OCT 1916
48th DIVISION.

Nature of Work.	Location of Work.	Progress of Work.	REMARKS.
ASSEMBLY TRENCHES.	**RIGHT SECTOR.**		**RIGHT SECTOR.**
Cleaning & boarding	B.	Repairs - ready for completion by trenchboards.	This trench is constantly shelled.
	C.	Serviceable throughout.	
	D.	Drainage complete - Trenchboards wanted.	Being deepened. Trenchboards required.
Digging.	E.	Trench full depth - YUSSIF to YOUNG.	Requires widening in one place, draining & trenchboarding.
COMMUNICATION TRENCHES.			
Cutting corner off	YIDDISH at HEB-FONQUEVILLERS Rd.	Trenchboards required.	
Cleaning & boarding	YIDDISH. FONQUEVILLERS Rd. to KERP.	200^x trenchboards required.	
Passing places.	NAP.	About 100^x widened as passing places in 3^x lengths at intervals of 20^x.	
Repair.	All Commn. trenches.	Permanent gangs. ~~Another day required.~~	More notice boards to be put up & trenchboards steadied.
RAILWAY.	LA HAIE-SOUASTRE RD. to BLUFF.	Another day required.	
TRENCHBOARD TRACK.	ditto. ditto.	Two days work left also 500^x trenchboards required.	
O.Ps.			
Construction (1)	YELLOW-R.	Finished.	
(2)	off YIDDISH.	Just begun.	
FORWARD DUMPS.			
Filling.	YOUNG & YELLOW	About half filled.	
ADVD. HD. QRS.			
Construction.	LA HAIE.	PROCEEDING.	
	LEFT SECTOR.		**LEFT SECTOR.**
COMMUNICATION TRENCHES.			
Improving, drainage, cleaning and firebays.	SIXTH ST..	2 drains improved, 2 more opened up. 3 Firebays cleaned.	Firebays will serve as passing places
Upkeep and repairs to trenchboards.	CALVAIRE.	Repaired throughout.	
ditto. ditto.	THORPE ST.	ditto.	
Cleaning, draining & boarding.	TUNNEL ST.	70^x cleaned and considerably deepened.	1 night to complete.
TUNNEL.	TUNNEL ST.	50' completed.(in all)	
TRAMLINE.	FONQUEVILLERS to TUNNEL ST.	New track laid from 6th STREET to where it is to cross THORPE St. (K.3.d.0.4.) Bridge made where it crosses MILL ST.	Track prepared for laying from K.3.d.0.4. to advanced R.E. dump TUNNEL ST. This will not be laid until night before Z.
SIGNAL O.P.	THORPE ST.	Seats and Tables made & fixed.	Complete.
DUGOUTS.			
SIGNAL SHELTER.	EBLE ST.	Completed	All 3 required are now completed.
Dugout for D/242	Nr. Bde. O.P.	Frames erected & sides revetted.	
SUNDRY R.E. WORK.		Trenches patrolled & repaired where necessary. Notice boards fixed. Notice & direction boards made, 2'6" trench bridges made. 20^x screen on FONQUEVILLERS-SOUASTRE Road thickened.	

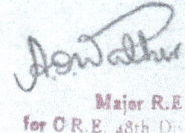

Major R.E.
for C.R.E. 48th D[iv]

DAILY WORK REPORT.

For 24 hours ending 6 a.m. 13-10-16.

Nature of Work.	Location of work.	Progress of work.	Remarks.
RIGHT SECTOR.	**RIGHT SECTOR.**		**RIGHT SECTOR.**
ASSEMBLY TRENCHES.			
Deepening and widening when needed.	E. Line.	Cleared and deepened except left quarter which was drained ready for clearing.	1 Coy can now finish in a night.
COMMUNICATION TRENCHES.			
Digging & sumping	YIDDISH.	1 day required	Sumps to be made & 60ˣ trenchboards required.
Widening	NAP.	Only ¼ done.	
Cleaning	All Commn. trenches.		Permanent parties.
OVERLAND TRACK.			
Fastening down trenchboards & preparing track.	BLUFF to LA HAIE.	No more can be done till trench boards for last 1000ˣ arrive.	Only 500ˣ trenchboards housed. Unboarded track being marked with white pickets
RAILWAY.			
Improving Permt. way & plate laying	BLUFF TO SOUASTRE RD.	Finished except for Mule track.	
O.Ps.			
Construction.	off YIDDISH.	4 or 5 days more needed	Useful work can go on for at least 10 days. 3 sappers only employed.
ADVD. H.Qrs.			
Construction.	LA HAIE	nearing completion.	Useful work can be done for some days in double bunking dug-outs to increase accommodation.
LEFT SECTOR.			**LEFT SECTOR.**
COMMUNICATION TRENCHES.			
Cleaning out firebays Improving drainage.	SIXTH ST.	3 firebays completed. 2 large sumps dug. Drain S. of Valley Avn. widened and 35ˣ boards laid	To serve as additional Commn. Trench.
Improving & repairing	MILL ST.	All sumps cleaned out Boards renewed where necessary.	
ditto.	THORPE ST.	Boards repaired throughout.	
Cleaning, draining & boarding.	TUNNEL ST.	Cleaned, deepened & boarded throughout.	Complete.
NEW TUNNEL.	CALVAIRE to TUNNEL ST.	67' completed	9' to complete
DUGOUTS.			
Dugout for D/242	Nr. Bde. O.P.	Sides revetted, roof fixed & 3' earth put on.	
Dugout & O.P. for A.& B./241	YIDDISH ST.	Work started 4-0 p.m.	
" " for A/240	R.Line	ditto.	
" " for A/243	E. of YANKEE ST.	ditto.	
" " for D/240	do.	ditto.	
" " for D/241	do.	ditto.	
" " for A/242	R.Mine	ditto.	
" " for B/242	E. of HADDON	ditto.	
" " for C/241	WOMAN ST.	ditto.	
ARTILLERY BRIDGES.			
Making ramps and approaches for artillery bridge.	K.19.a.	15ˣ of log ramp & approaches made each side of bridge (30ˣ in all)	Completed.
86" SCREEN			
Thickening screen.	FONQUEVILLERS-SOUASTRE ROAD.	50ˣ thickened and repaired.	
R.E.DUMPS.			
Various.		Filling with stores and Camouflaging.	
SUNDRY R.E.WORK.		Painting and fixing notice boards Making dugouts & O.P. frame. Assisting T.M.B. Etc., Etc.,	

R.E. HEAD QUARTERS
13 OCT 1916

A.D.Walker
Major R.E.
for C.R.E. 48th Div.

DAILY WORK REPORT.

For 24 hours ending 8-0 a.m. 14-10-16.

Nature of Work.	Location of Work.	Progress of Work.	REMARKS.
RIGHT SECTOR.	**RIGHT SECTOR.**		
ASSEMBLY TRENCHES.			
Cleaning	B.		
COMMUNICATION TRENCHES.			
Cleaning & repairs	All Comm. Trenches.	Permanent gangs.	
Sumping	YELLOW	Complete	
Cleaning & adjusting	VALLEY		Work delayed by prematures.
TRAMWAY.			
	LA HAIE.	Complete except for station at SOUASTRE end.	Begun to-day.
O.P.'s			
Construction	YANKEE		
ADVANCED DRESSING STATION.			
Preparing existing dugout, cutting ramps, etc.	SOLFERINO EAST.		
ADVANCED REPORT CENTRE.			
Construction, double bunking, etc.	LA HAIE.	Proceeding.	
LEFT SECTOR.		**LEFT SECTOR.**	
COMMUNICATION TRENCHES.			
Improving trench and cleaning out firebays.	SIXTH ST.	Drain S. of VALLEY Avn. completed as Comm. Trench. 3 large sumps dug in side of trench. 5 Firebays cleaned out.	
TUNNEL			
Deepening & revetting	TUNNEL ST.	Completed.	
New tunnel	CALVAIRE to TUNNEL ST.		Work hampered by 15 cms shell penetrating S. wall of tunnel 12' from entrance in CALVAIRE. The shell did not explode but R.E. Corporal was killed by direct hit. Very little damage done to tunnel.
DUGOUTS.			
Dugout for B/248	Near Bde. O.P.	Earth filled in & ready for bursting layer of logs.	
" & O.P. A.& B/241	YIDDISH ST.		
" " A/240	R. line W. of YANKEE ST.	Excavation for O.P. complete Framework made & carried to site.	
" " A/243	" " " " "	ditto.	
" " D/240	do.	ditto.	
" " D/241	do.	ditto.	
" " A/242	R. line E. of HADDON	ditto.	
" " B/242	" " " " "	ditto.	
" " C/241	WOMAN ST.	Excavation for O.P. complete & ready for O.P. framework.	
SCREENS.			
Thickening screen	FONQUEVILLERS-SOUASTRE Rd.	36 yds. thickened.	
TRAMWAY.			
Tramline	FONQUEVILLERS to TUNNEL ST.	Patrolled & repaired where necessary. Bridge made for crossing THORPE ST. Additional stores carried up.	
DUMPS.			

R.E. HEAD QUARTERS
No. 103.S.R.
14 OCT 1916
48th. DIVISION.

[signature]
Major R.E.
for C.R.E. 48th Div

DAILY WORK REPORT.

For 24 hours ending 6 a.m. 15-10-16.

Nature of Work.	Location of Work.	Progress of Work.	Remarks.
RIGHT SECTOR.		**RIGHT SECTOR.**	
ASSEMBLY TRENCHES.			
Digging.	Left of C.	Completed.	New length of trench for T.M Battery to prevent them having to deposit their ammunition C. trench.
Deepening & widening	E.	Completed – ready for T.B.	
COMMUNICATION TRENCHES.			
General repairs	All		Permanent parties.
Widening	NAP.	Proceeding	
Straightening	off YIDDISH.	Complete	For stretchers.
Cleaning, straightening & digging new approach.	VALLEY Trench.	Proceeding	Trenchboards to be moved to route & about 500^x extra req
Digging.	Railway crossing over FONQUEVILLERS-SAILLY Road.	Complete (100^x trench)	
RAILWAY.			
Addition of 50^x also station	Near end of railway.	Proceeding	6 carpenters supplied by 5th Sussex, working under R.E. Off
ADVANCED HD. QRS.			
Furniture, bunking, etc.	LA HAIE.		A new dugout is being made by G.O.C's desire to add to acco
DUMPS. Filling & repairing	YELLOW	Proceeding	
ADVANCED DRS. STATION.			
Approaches, etc.	SOLFERINO.	"	
EXPLOSIVE STORE. Construction.	CAT MILL.	Not yet complete.	
LEFT SECTOR.		**LEFT SECTOR.**	
COMMUNICATION TRENCHES.			
Clearing berm	KELLERMAN 6th STREET	Berm cleared for 350^x	Remainder night work.
Cleaning trench.	W. of THORPE ST.	70^x cleared between VALLEY Avn. & Bde. O.P.	
TUNNEL.			
New tunnel.	CALVAIRE to TUNNEL ST.	Completed.	Is now being improved by fitting intermediate cases
RAILWAY.			
Tramline	LA HAIE to BLUFF	200^x repaired & level crossings made.	
DUGOUTS.			
Dugout for D/242	Nr. Bde. O.P.	Casing fitted to exits, rough table made, bursting layer of logs placed on roof.	
Dugout & O.P. A.& B./241	YIDDISH ST.	Dugout frames erected and Excavation for exits made.	
do. do. A/240) A/243) D/240) D/241)	(R. line E. of (YANKEE ST. do.	O.P. framework fitted, rails for roof carried up. O.P. framework partly erected 8' gallery to dugout erected excavated & framed.	
A/242) B/242)	R. line E. of HADDON	Ready for O.P. framework. 8' gallery to dugout excavated & framed.	
C/241	WOMAN ST.	O.P. framework erected & rails for roof carried up. Sides revetted.	
R.E.DUMPS.		x Additional stores carried up.	
BELT WATER LIFTING GEAR.	SOUASTRE -S.22.a.6.8.	Erected. Horse troughs dismantled & partly erected.	1 day to complete.
SUNDRY R.E.WORK.		2 O.P. frameworks made. 8 gallery cases, 5'x2'6" made 12 Notice boards made & painted 12 rails cut for O.P. roofs. 2 men assisting on the T.M. emplacements.	

A.D.Walker.
Major R.E.
for C.R.E. 48th Div.

DAILY WORK REPORT.
For 24 hours ending 6 a.m. 16-10-16.

Nature of Work.	Location of Work.	Progress of Work.	Remarks.
FIRE TRENCHES.	**RIGHT SECTOR.**		**RIGHT SECTOR.**
Pumping & covering sumps with trenchboards, repairing	L. line.		
Repairing & boarding	B. line.		Left end.
Cleaning & sumping & joining up.	N.E. end of KEEP.	One more day required.	
COMMUNICATION TRENCHES.			
Trenchboarding & repairing	YIDDISH.	One more day required.	
Cleaning & moving trenchboards & digging new ends.	VALLEY Trench.	One more day when sufficient trenchboards have come.	
New cut.	B A Tunnel	One more night needed	This is a cut to prevent "Up" traffic to tunnel via YELLOW mixing with "Down" traffic from tunnel via YIDDISH.
Cleaning.	MAP.		
TRAMWAY.			
Station building	SOUASTRE RD.	2 days more needed.	
Construction.	off YIDDISH	proceeding.	
FIELD WORKS.			
Construction.	LA EYE.	"	
ADV'D DRS. STATION. (1)	SOLFERINO.	"	
(2)	G.Post LA HAIE.	"	
DUMPS.			
Repairs, camouflaging & filling.	YOUNG PURPLE & YELLOW.	Proceeding.	
	LEFT SECTOR.		**LEFT SECTOR.**
COMMUNICATION TRENCHES.			
Laying bays & cleaning out firebays.	RAILWAY & PLUG ST.	400 yds. completed. 8 firebays partly cleaned out.	
TUNNEL.			
New tunnel	CALVAIRE T. TUNNEL St.	Intermediate cases fitted throughout.	
DUGOUTS.			
Dugout for B/242	Bn. Hde. O.P.	Bursting layer completed over roof & covered with 12" earth.	1 day to complete entrances.
Dugout & O.P. for A.& B/241	YIDDISH St.	Logs fitted on dugout roof. Inside revetted & earth excavated for for entrance.	
ditto. for A/240 B/243	R. line S. of YAKUB St.	Rails fitted to roof, concreted and turfed over. O.P. frames braced.	
ditto. B/240 D/241	do.	O.P. framework partly erected. 2 cases fitted in gallery to dugout.	
ditto. A/242 B/243	R. line S. of HARROW.	2 cases reset owing to fall in roof. Excvn. for O.P. completed.	O.P. frame made & carried up.
ditto. C/241	WELSH St.	Entrance frames fitted sides revetted & O.P. frames braced.	
TRAMWAY.			
Mainline.	LA HAIE to PLUG	350 yds repaired & sleepers packed up.	
Mainline.	FONCQUEVILLERS to TUNNEL St.	3 new 15' sections put in owing to damage by shell fire. More stores carried up.	
DUMPS.			
WATER LIFTER.	SOUASTRE - H.25.a.8.3.	In working order, 20 yds. horse troughs erected.	30 yds more will be erected tomorrow = 400 horses per hour. Repairs to be made to road.
R.E. WORKS.		13 cases, 3'4" x 3'0" made. 11 " ditto. made. 2 " 3'0" x 2'4" 25 notice boards made & painted.	

16 OCT 1916
48th DIVISION.
1046RR

E. A. Sainsbury
Major R.E.
for C.R.E. 48th Div.

DAILY WORK REPORT.
For 24 hours ending 6 a.m. 17-10-16.

Nature of Work.	Location of Work.	Progress of Work.	Remarks.
RIGHT SECTOR.		**RIGHT SECTOR.**	
ASSEMBLY TRENCHES.			
Trenchboarding.	R. Left.	Completed.	
Deepening & widening	D. & E.	Proceeding.	To be finished to-day.
Cleaning, sumping & connecting to R.A.P.	S.T. of R.A.P.	Complete.	
COMMUNICATION TRENCHES.			
Construction.	From A. to B. & S. to YIDDISH Gap	Two more nights needed, work interfered with by weather.	(To facilitate meeting of "Up" (traffic along YELLOW & "Down" (traffic down YIDDISH at tunnel.
Sumping & trenchboarding	YIDDISH out across SET RI.	Complete.	
Raising bridge across trench	YIDDER - R.A.P.	"	
Trenchboarding	YIDDISH West.	One more day required.	
widening	NAP.	Proceeding.	
RAMP ROUTE (via VALLEY Trench)			
Cleaning & laying track of trenchboards.	LA HAIE to CAT HILL.	Proceeding - 1000' trenchboards required.	
RAILWAY.			
Improving track & laying chalk also quarrying.		Proceeding.	
Building Station.		3 days required.	
ADVANCED DRES. STATION.			
Construction of dugouts, etc. Approaches, etc.	SACKARDE BOLDCAINO.	Several days more to complete.	
ARTILLERY HD.QRS.			
Construction of dugouts, &c.	LA HAIE.	Proceeding.	
O.P.			
ditto. ditto.	off YIDDISH	"	
DRESSING STATION.			
Repairs, etc.	LA HAIE-s.		Complete.
BOMBS. Camouflaging sandbags.	Mr. TUNNEL	All inside A. line covered	Another night needed.
Making Bomb Store Preparing.	CAT HILL.	Complete.	
LEFT SECTOR.		**LEFT SECTOR.**	
COMMUNICATION TRENCHES.			
Cleaning out firebays	SIXTH ST.	3 dug to a depth of 4'6"	
Cutting passing places.	BALKEWAL	4 dug to an av. depth of 3'6", thrown up earth covered with grass	
Camouflaging sandbags.	MOUSETRAP	About 40' still to be done.	
TUNNEL.			
New tunnel	CALVAIRE to DUMMY ST.	Intermediate cases all fitted. CALVAIRE entrance sandbagged.	Complete.
TRAMWAY.			
	LA HAIE to DUMMY.	Chalk laid and rammed in for 250'.	
DUGOUTS.			
Dugout for 1/243	Rr. Bde. S.P.	Entrances revetted, floor boarded, table & bench fitted	Complete.
Dugout & O.P. A/241)	YIDDISH ST.	2 entrances to dugout completed earth excv. for O.P. framework.	
B/241)			
B/240)	F. Line S. of YARROW ST.	3 frames fitted to gallery. Back of O.P. revetted 3 frame cross braced.	
D/241)		Excvn. for O.P. complete, 2 cases fitted in gallery to dugout.	
A/242)	F. line S. of CAMDON.	5 frames fitted, 300 c.f. of earth excvt. and removed.	
B/243)			
C/241	ROMAN ST.	O.P. framework erected	
A/240)	F. line E. of YARROW ST.	6 cases fitted to gallery to dugout	
A/243)		20' Horse troughs erected.	
HARD WATER LISTED.	ROCASTRE-R.H.-s.&t.d.	85' of roadway made. Drain cut each side of road. 2 men assisting Q.T.?FCMC.	
ENEMY F.L. ...		Trenches patrolled & repaired, where necessary. 16 mining cases 5'x 2'6" made. 3 ditto. 5'x 5" " 1 O.P. framework completed. Notice boards made & painted. Seats & rails for O.P. made.	

R.E. HEAD QUARTERS
No.
17 OCT 1916
48th. DIVISION.

Major R.E.
for C.R.E. 48th Div

DAILY WORK REPORT.
For 24 hours ending 7 a.m. 18-10-16.

Nature of Work.	Location of Work.	Progress of Work.	Remarks.
RIGHT SECTOR.		**RIGHT SECTOR.**	
MAIN TRENCHES.			
Clean, sump & board	B. Line.	Complete	Requires continual repair owing to shell fire.
ditto.	C. Line.	170ˣ completed	To be completed by night of 18/19th.
ditto.	D. Line.		ditto. ditto.
COMMUNICATION TRENCHES.			
Cutting & boarding	A. to D. Br. TUNNEL	Interfered with by weather.	20 more men needed for one more night. No sumps made.
Cutting steps	YIDDISH.	8 steps made.	It is understood that no steps are required E. of SOHO-YER. Rd.
Branchboarding	"	Complete	
Repairs	All Commn. Trenches.		Permanent Parties.
Widening	MAP.		Two more days needed.
Boarding	VALLEY		Three more days & 1200ˣ french boards needed.
RAIL.			
Permanent way	SOUASTRE to LA BAZI.		Many days required to complete chalking the line.
Building station.	ditto.		2 days needed.
Construction.	off YIDDI.		6 days needed.
D.T.			
Bomb recesses	Forward Dumps.		2 days needed.
UNDERGROUND.			
New dugout & trench	LA BAZI		3 days needed.
Well head for water raiser			2 days needed.
Also clearing well.			
Sandbagging cellars			3 days needed.
Camouflaging debris	TUNNEL.		This should be done by Infantry clearing parties. It appears there is not proper reporting.
			their parties to enable I/c. I am inclined to think that 1 N.C.O. is not enough to run the tunnelling and direct the infantry.
LEFT SECTOR.		**LEFT SECTOR.**	
RAIL.	LA BAZI to REGNA.	Chalk laid along a further 150ˣ, line cleared ready for chalk for 3010ˣ.	
Div. O.P.	NAB ST.	Site cleared, front revetted, shaft sinking started.	
Bde. O.P.	YANKEE ST.	Bursting layer of bricks in sandbags laid on.	
DUGS.			
Dugout & O.P. for A/241 B/241	YIDDISH ST.	O.P. framework erected, sides revetted.	
ditto. A/240 B/241	R. line E. of YANKEE ST.	2 cases fitted in gallery.	
A/240	ditto.	Bunks, elbow rests, & shelf fitted in O.P. Gallery to dugout completed.	
D/241		O.P. framework adjusted.	
A/242 C/240	R. line E. of REDON.	2 cases fitted in gallery to dugout.	
C/241	YOKAI ST.	2 cases fitted.	No R.E. working party since 10-30 p.m. 16-10-16.
ROAD SUPPLY.	SOUASTRE-BRD.N.C.O.	20ˣ more road made.	
BLK QUARRYING.		10ˣ horse troughs erected.	
MISCY. R.E. WORK.		25 wagon loads quarried & carted away.	
		18 cases 2'x 4' made.	
		2 sump boxes made.	
		1 box drain, 15' long, made.	
		5 notice boards made & painted.	
		Tramlines patrolled.	
		Trenches patrolled.	
		2 men assisting I.M.B.	

R.E. HEADQUARTERS
No ......
18 OCT 1916
48th DIVISION.

H.M. Marshall
Lieut. & ad. Major R.E.
for C.R.E. 48th Div

R.E. HEAD QUARTERS
No. ....
19 OCT 1916

DAILY WORK REPORT.
For 24 hours ending 6 a.m. 19-10-16.

Nature of Work.	Location of Work.	Progress of Work.	Remarks.
ASSEMBLY TRENCHES.	RIGHT SECTOR.		RIGHT SECTOR.
Trenchboarding.	D.	Complete.	
Sumping.	E.	Nearly complete.	Trenchboards are in hand and should have been laid yesterday. They will be laid to-day – about 400ˣ.
COMMUNICATION TRENCHES.			
Repairs	YOUNG. YIDDISH. YELLOW.	Permanent Parties.	
Making steps	YIDDISH	3 complete.	
Widening	NAP.	Nearly finished	
Trenchboarding	VALLEY	Complete from top of hill S. of LA HAIE to CAT HILL.	
RAILWAY.			
Making roadway	LA HAIE	Just past the farm.	
O.P.			
Construction.	off YIDDISH	Proceeding.	
ADVANCED DRESSING STATION.			
Approaches.	SOLFERINO.	"	
ADVANCED HD. QRS.			
New dugout	LA HAIE	Proceeding	
Sandbagging cellar	"	Delayed by lack of materials.	
Paths	"		
Well head	"	Finish to-day	
	LEFT SECTOR.		LEFT SECTOR.
COMMUNICATION TRENCHES.			
Cleaning out firebays)	SIXTH ST.	3 firebays cleaned out.	
Fitting sump boxes)		2 sump boxes fitted.	
Digging passing places	KELLERMAN	Complete.	
Digging sumps.		3 large sumps dug.	
Cutting steps.		5 sets of steps cut out.	
Camouflaging sandbags.	CALVAIRE	About 30ˣ covered with earth	Most of this work rendered useless as fresh sandbags from the tunnels have been laid on top of the earth.
RAILWAY.		200ˣ relaid 120ˣ chalk laid	
Deepening, widening & revetting	TUNNEL ST.	30ˣ completed.	
O.P.			
Div. O.P.	NEW ST.	Vertical shaft sunk for 6' 4' of gallery at 45° excavated.	
DUGOUTS.			
Dugout & O.P. for A/241) B/241)	YIDDISH ST	Bursting layer of bricks laid on dugout. Rails on roof of O.P. concreted.	
A/240) A/243)	R. line S. of YANKEE ST.	1 gallery frame fitted, sides of gallery revetted, floor of O.P. boarded.	No R.A. working parties.
D/240) B/241)	ditto.	Rails on O.P. roof fixed.	
A/242) C/242)	R. line S. of HADDOCK.	O.P. framework erected, gallery to dugout sheeted top & sides.	
C/241	WOMAN STREET.	2 cases fitted in gallery. Rails laid on roof & concreted Loophole framework made, & ready to be fixed.	R.A. party by day only.
CHALK QUARRYING.	SQUAIRE.	20 wagon loads quarried & hauled away.	
WATER SUPPLY.	SQUAIRE. S.23.a.6.3.	10 yds. road made. Side drains revetted, 2 box drains made & laid. 10ˣ troughing erected. 30ˣ completed.	
SUNDRY R.E. WORK.		Tramline & trenches patrolled. 2 men assisting T.M.B. Large fall in THORPE ST. cleared. 2 sump boxes made. 6 mining cases 5' x 2'6" made. Fittings for O.P. & notice boards made Cover for belt water lifter made.	

A.D.Walker
Major R.E.
for C R E 48th Div

R.E. HEAD QUARTERS
No............
30 NOV 1916
48th. DIVISION.

CONFIDENTIAL.

WAR DIARY.

of

48th (South Midland) Divisional Engineers.

From 1st November 1916.........to.........30th November 1916.

(Volume 21.)

DAILY WORK REPORT.

For 24 hours ending 6 a.m. 20-10-16.

Nature of Work.	Location of Work.	Progress of Work.	Remarks.
RIGHT SECTOR.		**RIGHT SECTOR.**	
LEFT SECTOR.	No report received owing to move of 1st Field Coy.	**LEFT SECTOR.**	
COMMUNICATION TRENCHES. Digging large sumps, Completing & boarding passing places. Deepening.	KELLERMAN	Large sump dug every 100'. 2 passing places completed & boarded. Deepened 2' for 15' this side of overhead traverse.	
Deepening & boarding	CALVAIRE	Boarded throughout.	
	TUNNEL ST.		
RAILWAY.	FONQ. to TUNNEL ST.	Patrolled.	
O.P'S. Div. O.P.	TEMPLE ST.K.5.b.1.4.	Vertical shaft 4'6" x 2'6" sunk 5' leading to inclined gallery 12' of which is completed.	
Dugout & O.P.	YIDDISH ST.K.9.b.9.3.	Complete except for inside fittings, bench, table, etc.	
ditto.	R. line E. of YANKEE ST. K.10.a.8.0.	O.P. complete except for concrete on roof. Gallery 22' long complete. 2 cases in dugout chamber fitted.	
ditto.	R. line E. of YANKEE ST. K.10.c.60.95.	O.P. complete. Gallery 21'8" long complete, Excvn. for dugout started.	
ditto.	R. line E. of HADDON K.10.c.?.?	O.P. framework partly erected. Gallery 24' long complete, 1 case in dugout chamber fitted.	
ditto.	WOMAN ST. K.10.d.20.65.	O.P. complete. 23' gallery complete, dugout excvn. started.	

20 OCT 1916

Army Form C. 2118.

WAR DIARY
or
INTELLIGENCE SUMMARY.
(Erase heading not required.)

Instructions regarding War Diaries and Intelligence Summaries are contained in F. S. Regs., Part II. and the Staff Manual respectively. Title pages will be prepared in manuscript.

Place	Date	Hour	Summary of Events and Information	Remarks and references to Appendices
MILLENCOURT.	1916. Nov. 1.		At MILLENCOURT.	
	2.		1/1st S.M. Field Co. R.E. moved to BAZENTIN CAMP.	
	3.		R.E. Hd. Qrs. moved to LOZENGE WOOD. 48th Division relieved 15th Division.	
	4.		1/2nd S.M. Field Co. R.E. Hd. Qrs. and 3 Sections moved to SHELTER WOOD, and one section to MARTINPUICH.	
	5-30.		See attached work reports.	

Major R.E.,
For C.R.E., 48th Division.

H/31 R.E.

48th DIVISION.

PROGRESS REPORT FOR 24 HOURS ENDING NOON 30-11-16.

WILLIAM ALLEY. - 100 men working & trench passable to SPENCE TRENCH.

GILBERT ALLEY. - 200 men digging big sump.

DUGOUTS.

    BATTN. H.Q.) - 36 ft. driven - 50 loads frames carried to site.
    GILBERT ALLEY)

    O.G.1.   - 65% done.

    LE SARS   - No progress as carrying party with materials did not arrive.

BOMB STORES.

    LE SARS   - Completed.

DIV. R.E. DUMP,) - 9 trucks stores sent from CONTALMAISON.
MARTINPUICH   )

TRAMWAYS.

    VILLA STATION SIDING. - Road completed - levelling & laying 60 yds track.

    SOUTHERN BRANCH.   - 60 sleepers cut and laid.
                                150 yds formation prepared.

    VILLA WOOD   - 54 yds rail laid - 70 yds ballasted.

    WAGON SIDING   - 24ft platform revetment done.
    A.17.b.53.

TRENCHBOARD TRACKS.

    MARTINPUICH - EAUCOURT - 133 yds boards made.
                                    Track completed to M.27.b.72.

    TO LEFT SECTOR.   - Track laid from R.E. Dump to GUNPIT ALLEY at M.31.b.09.
                              25 boards made - 185 boards laid.
                              200 yds boards fixed.

    INFANTRY TRACK.   - 350 yds laid. Head of track now 150 yds short of CONTALMAISON VILLA - MARTINPUICH Track.

HUTTING.   DIV'L H.Q. - R.A. Mess - Frame commenced.

            MOTOR GARAGE - 20ft chalk laid.
                            20ft road   "
                            Completing rafters & purlins - laying C.I. begun.

            STAGE FOR DIV'L) - 30% completed.
            CURIOS - A.21.b.90)

            NISSEN HUT CAMPS. - Completed except for fencing, drains latrines etc.

R.E. DUMP. Trench pathway of) 1800' completed.
           wire netting & stakes) Total 5,100'

                                          A.O. Walker
                                              Major R.E.
30-11-16.   for C.R.E., 48th Division.

48th DIVISION.

PROGRESS REPORT FOR 24 HOURS ENDING NOON 29-11-16.

GILBERT ALLEY. — Digging sumps.

DUGOUTS.

    BATTN. H.Q.) — 33ft driven — Frames carried to site.
    GILBERT ALLEY.)

    O.G.1.   — 59% done.

    LE SARS   — 61 frames in — 50 loads frames carried up.

BOMB STORES.

    LE SARS   — 60 % done.

DIV. R.E. DUMP   — 12 loads stores sent from CONTALMAISON.
MARTINPUICH.

TRAMWAYS.

    VILLA STATION) — Levelling ground & draining 15ft road laid — hauling
    SIDING.   )   sleepers.

    SOUTHERN BRANCH. — 40 yds rail laid — 100 sleepers prepared & laid —
                              level crossing made at M.33.b.97 — 200 yds new track
                              completed.
                              Railhead — Bde. H.Q.

    VILLA WOOD.   — Completed from X.17.b.53 to X.12.c.56.

    WAGON SIDING) — Side of platform revetted for 84ft — 40ft revetment
    X.17.b.53.   )   anchored.

TRENCHBOARD TRACKS.

    MARTINPUICH-EAUCOURT. 156 ft. boards made.
                                  200 yds track dumped at bottom of WILLIAM ALLEY —
                                  40 yds laid in parapet up WILLIAM ALLEY.

    GILBERT ALLEY.   — 20 boards made, laid & fixed.

    INFANTRY TRACK. — 400 yds laid. Head of track now 500 yds. N. of
                                POZIERES — BAZENTIN-le-PETIT road & running
                                parallel to MARTINPUICH — BAZENTIN ROAD.

HUTTING.

    DIV. H.Q. — R.A. office — Work done on partitions & lining.
                No. 2 & 3 Messes   "   "   " lining.
                   ditto.   Cookhouse nearly completed.
                R.A. Mess —   Laying out.
                MOTOR GARAGE —   10ft chalk laid.
                                     15ft road "
                                     Levelling ground — Fitting wall plates
                                     & rafters.

BAZENTIN CAMPS. — Nissen huts practically completed, fencing, drains,
                         latrines, etc. in hand.

R.E. DUMP. — Trench pathway of wire) 1800 ft. completed.
          netting & stakes.   ) (3300 ft. since yesterday morning.)

                                                                   Major R.E.
29-11-16.   for C.R.E., 48th Division.

48th DIVISION.

PROGRESS REPORT FOR 24 HOURS ENDING NOON 28-11-16.

1597 RE

GILBERT ALLEY. — Digging sumps ~~500 cu. yds.~~

DUGOUTS.

    BATTN. H.Q.   — 30 ft. driven.
    GILBERT ALLEY.

    O.G.1   — 56 ft. driven — 66% done.

    LE SARS   — 53 frames fixed, 50 loads frames & C.I. carried to site.

BOMB STORES.

    LE SARS.   — 60% done.

    CRESCENT ALLEY — 60% done.

DIV. R.E. DUMP)   — 65 men collecting material.
MARTINPUICH.)   12 loads stores sent from CONTALMAISON.

TRAMWAYS.

    VILLA STATION SIDING. — Making drains for road & making up ground for tramline permanent way.

    SOUTHERN BRANCH — 120 yds rail laid — Bridge completed at M.32.b.97. Remainder of rails transported from BAZENTIN Station to railhead. Railhead M.33.a.18.
                                   220 yds track prepared, commencing from CRESCENT ALLEY Station — 140 yds rails placed in position.

    VILLA WOOD.   — 25 yds rail laid (525 yds to date)

    WAGON SIDING) — 12 double fascines laid.
    AT X.17.b.63.)   clearing of earth completed.

TRENCHBOARD TRACKS.

    MARTINPUICH-EAUCOURT — 48ft boards made & dumped at M.27.c.95 — 185 boards carried, from this dump to WILLIAM ALLEY. 16 yds brick track relaid. Track completed to M.22.c.83.

    GILBERT ALLEY. — 20 boards made and laid. Collecting material and repairing track. Track completed to M.15.a.51.

    INFANTRY TRACK. — 400 yds boards laid. Head of track now about 100 yds beyond BAZENTIN — POZIERES Road.

HUTTING.   — Equivalent of 15 huts erected.

    SOUP KITCHEN NEAR) — Practically completed.
    VILLA STATION   )

    DIV. H.Q.   — R.A. Hut — Flooring and lining.
                        No. 2 & 3 Messes — Lining & cookhouse commenced.

                  MOTOR GARAGE. — Quarrying chalk, preparing site for road.
                                          Roofing of Garage commenced.

R.E. DUMP. — Trench pathway completed of wire netting & stakes.

48th DIVISION.

PROGRESS REPORT FOR 24 HOURS ENDING NOON 27-11-16.

DUGOUTS.

    O.G.1. — 54' driven - cleaning and draining trench adjoining 20 loads frames carried up.

    NEW BATTN. H.Q. — 23' driven - 80 loads frames carried up.
    GILBERT ALLEY.

    LE SARS. — Salvaging frames from old dugouts & 50 loads frames carried up.

BOMB STORES.

    SUNKEN ROAD — 25% done.
    LE SARS.

    CRESCENT ALLEY. — 30% done - drained and cleaned trench adjoining.

DIV. R.E. STORE — 100 men collecting stores.
MARTINPUICH.
    2 loads stores sent from CONTALMAISON - by night.
    12 "   "   "   " CONTALMAISON - by day.

TRAMWAYS.

    VILLA STATION SIDING. — 100 fascines laid & shell holes filled in.

    SOUTHERN BRANCH. — 150 yds rail laid
        80 yds dogs fixed.
        100 sleepers prepared.
        130 yds of rails taken from BAZENTIN to VILLA Station.
        150 yds. new track prepared.
        300 yds. track previously done improved.
        Railhead M.33.a.18.

    VILLA WOOD, — 50 yds rail laid - 150 yds ballasted.
        100 yds. boards laid.
        Wagon siding at X.17.b.53 continued.

TRENCHBOARD TRACKS.

    MARTINPUICH-EAUCOURT — 165ft boards made.
        Track diverted at M.32.d.45 for 80 yds.
        16 yds brick track laid.
        Shelter for permanent party commenced at at M.27.b.89.

    GILBERT ALLEY. — 35 yds boards made.

    INFANTRY TRACK. — 350 yds boards laid.
        Complete from O.G. to BAZENTIN-POZIERES Rd.

HUTTING.
    GORDON CAMP   )
    BDE. H.Q. CAMP   ) Equivalent of 16 huts
    SCOTS REDOUBT CAMP N.) erected.
      "   "   " S.)

    ERECTION OF SOUP KITCHEN)   25% done.
    Near VILLA STATION.   )

    DIV'L H.Q. — R.A. Hut - Flooring & lining.
        A.D.M.S. hut - Completed.
        Amiens hut for "G" Clerks - Nearly complete.

P.T.O.

HUTTING (Continued).

    DIV'L H.Q.   No. 2 & 3 Messes - Lining & partitioning.
    (continued)

    MOTOR GARAGE. - Remaining uprights erected - quarrying chalk & filling in shell holes.

    DIV. BOMB SCHOOL. - Fitting up.

    R.A. TRANSPORT LINES. - Marking out.

27-11-16.

                                        Major R.E.
                                  for C.R.E., 48th Division.

1556 R.E.

48th DIVISION.

PROGRESS REPORT FOR 24 HOURS ENDING NOON 26-11-16.

WILLIAM ALLEY. No work possible owing to depth of water & the fallen earth in the trench.

GILBERT ALLEY. Sumps dug in 500 yds of trench.

DUGOUTS.

    O.G.1. – Trench cleaning & removing sandbags) No Infantry for
    NEW BATTN H.Q. – 17ft driven.) these works have
    GILBERT ALLEY.) reported since 23rd inst.

BOMB STORES – 70th TRENCH – 90% done.

DIV. R.E. DUMP, 100 men collecting stores.
MARTINPUICH. 12 trucks stores sent from CONTALMAISON.

TRAMWAYS:-

    VILLA STATION SIDING. – 30' roadway laid – shell holes filled in etc.

    SOUTHERN BRANCH. – 90 sleepers prepared.
    Packing of sleepers continued.
    200 yds. new track prepared.
    75 yds of rail taken from VILLA STATION to railhead.
    Railhead at M.32.b.97.

    VILLA WOOD. – 75 yds rail laid.
    100 yds poling boards laid, single run.
    100 yds ballasted.
    Wagon siding X.17.b.53.
    10 yds. of fascines laid, cutting extended. 10 yds.

TRENCHBOARD TRACK.

    MARTINPUICH-EAUCOURT. – 80 yds track relaid from N.W. to S.E. side of new tramway in M.32.d..
    18 yds. of brick track relaid.

    GILBERT ALLEY. – 100 trenchboards carried & laid.
    Track completed to M.15.c.51.

    INFANTRY TRACK) 180 yds trenchboards laid.
    X.17.b.93 to S.2.c.53.)

HUTTING. – Unloading material & distribution of same over Shelter Wood Camp – lining of huts.
Owing to bad weather the Infantry were not employed for the full time.

    DIV. H.Q:- Erecting Amiens hut.
    Flooring R.A. hut.
    Commenced lining No. 2 & 3 Mess hut.

    MOTOR GARAGE. Quarrying chalk, erecting frames and filling in shell holes.

26-11-16.

Major R.E.
for C.R.E., 48th Division.

48th DIVISION.

PROGRESS REPORT FOR 24 HOURS ENDING NOON 25-11-16.

1543 RE

WILLIAM ALLEY:- Making sumps for drainage.
Clearing trench from ~~~~~~ to FLERS Line.

GILBERT ALLEY:- Cleaning and widening up to DESTREMONT FARM.

DUGOUTS:-

    O.G.1. — 52% completed.

    SUNKEN RD.-LE SARS — Frames carried to dugout & tunnellers fixing same.

    NEW BATTN. H.Q. — Shaft 16ft. - Frames carried.

CRESCENT ALLEY:- — 80 yds. cleared & berms made.

**BOMB STORES -
SPENCE TRENCH:-
M.28.a.36.** — 1 shelter completed with framework & roof.

BOMB STORE, 70th TRENCH:- 30% completed.

**BOMB STORE, SUNKEN RD.-
LE SARS:-** 10% completed.

**DIV. R.E. DUMP,
MARTINPUICH:-** 95 men collecting stores.
12 trucks stores sent from CONTALMAISON.

TRAMWAYS.

    VILLA SIDING:- 120 fascines drawn & delivered to site to complete road.

    SOUTHERN BRANCH:- Railhead M.32.b.9565.
195 yds dog spikes fixed.
100 sleepers prepared.
Work on bridge continued.
Packing of sleepers continued.
200 yds new track prepared.
40 lengths of rail stripped from CRESCENT ALLEY branch.
150 yds rail laid roughly in new alignment.

    VILLA WOOD:- 25 yds. ballasted & boarded.
25 yds rails laid.
Sandbag retaining wall made in large shell hole.
1 truck made.

TRENCHBOARD TRACKS.

    MARTINPUICH-EAUCOURT:- By night - 150 trenchboards carried from M.27.c.95 to WILLIAM ALLEY & from M.22.c.33 forward.
By Day. - Laying boards in WILLIAM ALLEY & repairing track.
Track completed to M.22.c.33.

    GILBERT ALLEY:- 27 trenchboards made & dumped.
Track completed to M.21.a.37.

P.T.O.

2.

HUTTING.	Gordon Camp,)	
	Bde. H.Q. Camp,)	Equivalent of
	Scots Redoubt N.Camp,)	16 huts erected.
	" " S.")	
	Shelter Wood Camp.)	

Div'l H.Q:- "G" Extension - Completed.

R.A. Hut - Weather boarding sides.

Motor Garage &) 10ft sheding erected.
road for wagons) Filling in shell holes on new road.

R.E. DUMP.   Making oil drum stoves, checking stores and general store work.

25-11-16.

Major R.E.
for C.R.E., 48th Division.

48th DIVISION.

PROGRESS REPORT FOR 24 HOURS ENDING NOON 24-11-16.

91st Fld. Co.	WILLIAM ALLEY.	Deepening gun drains & making sump pits.
1st Fd. Co.	GILBERT ALLEY.	Cleaning & widening. Trenchboards laid from BAPAUME ROAD to 150 yds. W. of DESTREMONT FARM.
91st Fd. Co.	BOMB SHELTER M.28.a.36.	40 yds. trench deepened to 5ft.
	CRESCENT ALLEY.	Cleared 50 yds. of trench from M.27.b.7½

Dugouts

1st Fd. Co. (1)	O.G.1.	50 ft. done - 50 ft more to do. Frames carried to site.
do. (2)	SUNKEN RD.-LE SARS.	2 shafts down 20 ft. 1 shaft " 6 ft.
do. (3)	NEW BATTN. H.Q.	1 shaft " 12 ft.
do.	DIV. R.E. DUMP - MARTINPUICH.	65 men collected stores.
do.	4 WATER TANKS - GUNPIT ROAD.	Completed.
2nd Fd. Co.	FORWARD TRAMWAY.	
	VILLA STATION SIDING.	Levelling for line. Making up surface of corduroy & digging drain.
5th Sussex.	SOUTHERN BRANCH.	Railhead M.32.b.85. 230 yds. rails laid - 130 yds dogs fixed. 150 yds sleepers prepared. Work continued on Bridge at M.32.b.97. 400 yds of permanent way removed from HIGH WOOD-CRESCENT ALLEY line.
91st Fd. Co.	VILLA WOOD.	175 yds ballasted - Formation now prepared to VILLA WOOD. 100 yds. straight & 50 yds. curve laid. 200 yds. boards laid on track. Preparing wagon siding at A.17.b.53.

TRENCHBOARD TRACKS.

5th Sussex.	MARTINPUICH-EAUCOURT -	By night - 270 yds trenchboards carried from M.27.c.95 to WILLIAM ALLEY & from M.27.b.99 forward. By day. Laying trenchboards in WILLIAM ALLEY & repairing track. Track completed to M.22.c.33.
5th Sussex.	GILBERT ALLEY. -	50 trenchboards made. Track completed to M.21.a.37.
9th Gordons.	HUTTING, Gordon Camp.) Bde. H.Q. Camp.) Scots Redoubt N.) " " S.) Shelter Wood.)	Equvalent of 14 huts erected.
2nd Fd. Co.	DIV. H.Q.	"G" extension) Completed and lined. O.R.E's Mess)

2nd Fd.Co.	HUTTING (Continued) DIV. H.Q.	"A" & "Q" Hut. Complete except a few fittings. Making porch. R.A. Hut. - Work on roofing.
1st.Fd.Co.	DIV. BATHS. -	80% completed. Ready for bathing troops.
2nd Fd.Co.	R.E.DUMP. -	Erecting Sawmill. Tramway completed.

A O Walker

Major R.E.
for C.R.E., 48th Division.

24-11-16.

48th DIVISION.

PROGRESS REPORT FOR 24 HOURS ENDING NOON 23.11.16.

1516 R.E.

91st Field Co. R.E.	WILLIAM ALLEY.	60 yds. trench prepared and 40 yds. boards laid up to M.27.b.78.
1st Field Co. R.E.	GILBERT ALLEY.	500 yds. cleared and widened.
91st Field Co. R.E.	BOMB STORES, SPENCE TRENCH.	Excavation completed.
1st Field Co. R.E.	BOMB SHELTERS, 70th TRENCH.	50% completed.
do.	DUGOUTS.	
do.	O.G.1.	Horizontal drive now 20 ft. long. New shaft 6 ft. down
do.	New Bttn. Hd.Qrs.	Shaft 8 ft. down.
do.	Sunken Road - Le Sars.	2 shafts down 18 ft. 3rd shaft started. Old German shafts cleared out and horizontal dugouts continued. 100 men carrying dugout timber to this place.
1st Field Co. R.E.	DIV. R.E. DUMP, MARTINPUICH.	65 men collecting material. 12 trucks stores received from CONTALMAISON.
	FORWARD TRAMWAY.	
2nd Field Co. R.E.	Villa Station siding -	Filling in shell holes and preparing ground for tramline; taking up one set of points and fixing in new position.
5th Sussex.	Southern Branch.	220 yds. rail laid. 250 sleepers prepared. Track prepared to M.33.a.29 Bridge at M.32.b.97 continued. Dog spikes fixed for 75 yds. Material carried.
91st Field Co. R.E.	Villa Wood.	160 yds. track laid. 50 " " formation continued. 150 " " ballasted. 110 " rough boarding put on centre of track.
	TRENCHBOARD TRACKS.	
5th Sussex.	MARTINPUICH-EAUCOURT.	83 yds. boards made. Track completed to M.27.b.99.
do.	GILBERT ALLEY.	38 trenchboards made and dumped. Track completed to M.21.a.37.
91st Field Co. R.E.	INFANTRY TRACK. (X.17.b.93 - S.7.b.97)	Completed but not trenchboarded.
	VILLA STATION - MARTINPUICH.	30 yds. completed and joined to existing track.

HUTTING.

9th Gordon Highlanders.	Gordon Camp.	Stables 80% completed. Medical hut 40% completed.
do.	Bde. H.Q. Camp.)	
do.	Scots Redoubt Camp. S.)	Equivalent of 16 huts erected.
do.	do. N.)	
do.	Shelter Wood Camp.)	
2nd Field Co. R.E.	Div. Hd. Qrs. - "G" extension.) "C.R.E's Mess".) "A & Q" hut. "R.A." hut. Motor garage.	Lining interiors and putting in stove. Work on fittings. Completing frame. Erecting uprights for shedding.
1st Field Co. R.E.	Div. Baths.	77% completed.

R.E. DUMP.

2nd Field   General store work.
Co. R.E.   Making stoves.
               Completing hutting.
               Making bed for engine.

23.11.16.

Major R.E.
For C.R.E., 48th Division.

48th DIVISION.

1501 R.E.

PROGRESS REPORT FOR 24 HOURS ENDING NOON 22-11-16.

WILLIAM ALLEY.   Laying trench boards continued.

GILBERT ALLEY.   Continued, clearing, widening & relaying trenchboards.

BOMB SHELTERS:-
70th TRENCH & SUNKEN RD.,
LE SARS.   ) Continued.

NEW LEFT BATTN. HD. QRS.
DUGOUT - M.21.c.27.   Progressing.

DUGOUTS IN O.G.1.   do.

DUGOUT IN SUNKEN ROAD IN LE SARS.   do.

WORK IN MARTINPUICH.   Saw erected & working, and 12 loads material collected.

FORWARD TRAMWAY.

    VILLA STATION. - Corduroy road to platform - nearly half completed.
                         Laying tramline loop-commenced.

    SOUTHERN BRANCH. -120 yds rail laid.
                         300 " track prepared.
                         Bridge at M.32.b.97 continued.
                         150 sleepers prepared.
                         Material carried.

TRENCHBOARD TRACKS.

    MARTINPUICH-EAUCOURT.   117 yds. boards made.
                                    50 yds carried to dump.
                                 Track repaired and re-bricked.

    GILBERT ALLEY.   40 trenchboards made & dumped.
                         Track laid to M.21.a.37.

    TRANSPORT TRACK.   300 yds formation prepared.
                         100 yds. rail laid on wooden sleepers.

    VILLA STATION.   300 yds. boards laid.

HUTTING.   Bde. Hd. Qrs. Camp   ) Equivalent of 16
               Scots Redoubt Camp S.)
               " " " N.) huts erected.

              Div'l Hd. Qrs.   G. extension & C.R.E's mess 50% completed.
                                   Motor Garage - continued.

              Div'l Baths.   -   75% completed.

R.E. DUMP.   Siding completed.
                20 ft. corduroy required to complete road.
                Tramway practically completed.

22-11-16.

                                                           Major R.E.
                                            for C.R.E., 48th Division.

48th DIVISION.

PROGRESS REPORT FOR 24 HOURS ENDING NOON 21-11-16.

WILLIAM ALLEY. 90^X trench cleared.
                 100^X trenchboards laid.
                 New drain 40^X long made.

GILBERT ALLEY.   Work on cleaning, widening & relaying trenchboards.

NEW LEFT BATTN. H.Q.   Site chosen in GILBERT ALLEY at M.20.d.84
DUGOUT-M20.d.84.   & work started.

DUGOUTS IN O.G.1.   Continued.

DUGOUT IN SUNKEN ROAD   Continued.
LE SARS.

WORK IN MARTINPUICH.   12 loads material collected.
                 Erecting water tanks at GUNPIT ROAD.

FORWARD TRAMWAY.

     VILLA STATION. - Work continued on siding.

     NORTHERN BRANCH.- Relaying board track along N. boundary
                 of tramlines.

     SOUTHERN BRANCH.- Track partly prepared for 400^X.
                 40^X rail laid.
                 100^X sleepers prepared.
                 Bridge at M.32.b.97 commenced.
                 Material carried.

VILLA WOOD TRAMWAY.   Work done on making bends & collecting
                 material ready for laying.

TRENCHBOARD TRACKS.

     MARTINPUICH-EAUCOURT. - 160^X boards made.
                 63^X carried to dump.
                 Track repaired & re-bricked.

     GILBERT ALLEY. - 40 trenchboards made & dumped.

     TRANSPORT TRACK. - Bridge near BAZENTIN WOOD
                 completed.
                 4 Notice boards erected & some
                 pickets painted.

HUTTING.   Bde. H.Q. Camp.) - Equivalent of 12
          Scots Redoubt   )
          Camp S.   )   huts erected.

          Div'l Hd.Qrs. - Work continued on "A" & "Q" Office.
                         "   "   " "G" extension.
                       Motor Garage - Cutting completed.
                       "   "   Shedding commenced.

          MotorCycle Siding.
          at X.17.b.72.   Completed.

          Div'l Baths.   73% completed.

R.E. DUMP.   Work on store and laying tramline continued.

                               Major R.E.
21-11-16.   for C.R.E., 48th Division.

48th DIVISION.

PROGRESS REPORT FOR 24 HOURS ENDING NOON 20-11-16.

WILLIAM ALLEY. 200^X cleared on old parts where trench has fallen in.

GILBERT ALLEY. Work continued on cleaning and widening.

BOMB SHELTERS:-
70th TRENCH & SUNKEN RD.,) Continued, 10% done.
LE SARS.

NEW BATTN. HD. QRS.) Stopped - new site being chosen by Bde.
DUGOUT -M.21.c.27.)

DUGOUTS IN O.G.1   Continued.

SUNKEN ROAD IN LE SARS. Dugouts continued.

WORK IN MARTINPUICH. Materials collected.

FORWARD TRAMWAY. 100^X track prepared & sleepers cut ready.
(Southern Branch)
VILLA WOOD TRAMWAY. 170^X formation prepared.
Rails collected & bends made as required.

TRENCHBOARD TRACKS.

MARTINPUICH-EAUCOURT. 139^X of boards made & carried to dumps at M.27.c.95.

GILBERT ALLEY. 14 trenchboards made & large supply of material collected.

TRANSPORT TRACK. Track formation completed from S.7.b.97. to S.2.c.53.

HUTTING. Bde. Hd. Qrs. Camp.) Equivalent of 10
Scots Redoubt Camp.S.) huts erected.

Div'l Hd. Qrs. Work done on A.& Q. offices.
"   "   "   G. extension.

Motor cycle siding.) Levelled out and corduroy floor
X.17.b.72   ) completed.

Siding -VILLA Station. Continued.

Drawing of huts from) 7 complete Nissen Huts &
BAZENTIN SIDING.   ) woodwork of 9 others drawn.

Div'l Baths. 70% completed.

R.E.DUMP. Making corduroy siding & laying tramline.

20-11-16.

Major R.E.
for C.R.E., 48th Division.

1467 R.E.

48th DIVISION.

PROGRESS REPORT FOR 24 HOURS ENDING noon 19.11.16.

WILLIAM ALLEY.	150 yds. cleared. 110 yds. trenchboards put in and steps made at entrance to trench by EAUCOURT L'ABBAYE.
GILBERT ALLEY.	Work on clearing, widening and relaying trench boards.
BOMB SHELTERS in 70th Trench & Sunken Road, LE SARS. Continued.	
DUGOUTS in O.G.1.	Continued.
New Bttn. Hd.Qrs. M.21.c.27.	Continued.
SUNKEN ROAD, LE SARS.	Work on dugouts continued.
WORK IN MARTINPUICH.	Road through village. Completed from W. end of village to M.27.c.53. 12 truck loads stores collected.
FORWARD TRAMWAY.	Maintained

TRENCHBOARD TRACKS.

MARTINPUICH-EAUCOURT.	473 ft. boards made & dumped.
GILBERT ALLEY.	38 trenchboards and 200 pickets made.
TRANSPORT TRACK.	100 yds. track formation made. Loop to VILLA Hd. Qrs. completed. Work done on improving track from X.17.b.93. to MIDDLE WOOD.
VILLA STATION, MARTINPUICH.	Pioneer rest day.

HUTTING. Acid Drop Camp, S.) Pioneer Camp.) Gordon Camp.) Bde. H.Q. Camp.) Scots Redoubt Camp, S.)	Pioneer rest day.
Div. Hd. Qrs.	Completing "A" and "G" offices and putting in windows. Motor garage continued.
Road siding at VILLA STATION.	Work continued.
Div. Baths.	67½% completed.
R.E. DUMP.	Work on cutting of siding and laying tramline continued. Point put in and connection made with main line.

Major R.E.
For C.R.E., 48th Divn.

19.11.16.

48th DIVISION.

PROGRESS REPORT FOR 24 HOURS ENDING NOON 18 - 11 - 16.

WILLIAM ALLEY.   150^X completed.

GILBERT ALLEY.   Work done on clearing and widening.

BOMB SHELTER.   70th Trench & Sunken Road commenced.

DUGOUTS in O.G.1   Continued.

     New Battn. H.Q.) Continued.
     M.21.c.27.   )

SUNKEN ROAD IN LE SARS.   2 shafts dug 12ft into bank, cover obtained 10ft.

WORK IN MARTINPUICH.   Road through village completed from S.W. end of village to M.27.c.0505. 12 loads material collected.

FORWARD TRAMWAY.   No party available as they had to be employed carrying Nissen Huts.

TRENCHBOARD TRACKS.

     MARTINPUICH-EAUCOURT.   145^X boards made, track repaired where necessary.

     GILBERT ALLEY.   Boards laid to M.21.a.37.

     TRANSPORT TRACK.   200^X track formation made. Bridge near BAZENTIN WOOD completed.

     VILLA STATION   188^X boards laid.
     MARTINPUICH.

HUTTING.   ACID DROP CAMP S.)
             PIONEER CAMP.   )
             GORDON CAMP.   ) Work continued.
             BDE. H.Q. CAMP.)
             SCOTS REDOUBT S.)

          DIV'L H.Q.   "G" and "Q" hut extension & Motor Garage continued.

          ROAD SIDING AT   15ft corduroy relaid.
          VILLA STATION.

          DIV'L BATHS.   65% completed.

G.O.C's MOTOR CAR SIDING.   Completed.
     X.17.b.72.

R.E.DUMP.   Work continued on cutting of siding & laying tramline.

A.O.Walker.

Major.R.E.,

18-11-16.   for C.R.E., 48th Division.

R.E. HEAD QUARTERS
No. 1442 R.E.
17 NOV 1916
48th DIVISION.

48th/DIVISION.

PROGRESS REPORT FOR 24 HOURS ENDING NOON 17.11.16.

WILLIAM ALLEY.   200 yds. completed.

GILBERT ALLEY.   Work on clearing and pumping continued.

BOMB STORE,   Completed.
26th Avenue.

DUGOUTS IN O.G.1.   Continued.

New Bttn. H.Q.   Commenced.
in M.21.c.27.

SUNKEN ROAD- LE SARS.   Work on dugouts continued.

WORK IN MARTINPUICH.   Road through village. - 170 yds. prepared.
    230 yds. completed.
Material collected, 7 loads.

FORWARD TRAMWAY.   No party available as they were employed carrying Nissen huts.

TRENCHBOARD TRACKS:

    MARTINPUICH-EAUCOURT.   375 ft. boards made. 270 yds. laid.

    GILBERT ALLEY.   400 bearers made and boards carried.

    TRANSPORT TRACK.   100 yds. formation made.
Chalk and flint put in bad places.
Bridge by corner of BAZENTIN WOOD 75% completed.

    VILLA STATION,   400 yds. of boards laid.
    MARTINPUICH.

HUTTING.   Acid Drop Camp, S.)
    Pioneer Camp.)
    Gordon Camp.)
    Brigade H.Q. Camp,)   Equivalent of 16 huts erected.
      Shelter Wood.)
    Scots Redoubt Camp.)

    Div. Hd. Qrs.   Work on "G" hut and motor garage continued.

    Platform & road at   Work on road continued.
    VILLA STATION.

    Div. Baths.   60% completed.

R.E. DUMP.   Cutting out of siding continued.

48th DIVISION.

PROGRESS REPORT FOR 24 HOURS ENDING noon 16 - 11 - 16.

> R.E. HEAD QUARTERS
> No 1424 R.E.
> 16 NOV 1916

WILLIAM ALLEY (M.22.c. to M.22.c.43)	No Infantry party reported to-day.
GILBERT ALLEY.	Pumping & cleaning preparatory to trench boarding.
BOMB STORE. 26th Avenue.	Continued.
DUGOUTS in O.G.1.	Continued.
SUNKEN ROAD IN LE SARS.	Work on Dugouts and roads continued.
WORK IN MARTINPUICH.	Road through village - 172^X prepared - 162^X completed. 6 loads material collected.
FORWARD TRAMWAY.	105^X sleepers laid.

TRENCHBOARD TRACKS.

MARTINPUICH-EAUCOURT.	- 431 ft. boards made and repairs done to track laid.
GILBERT ALLEY.	- 600 bearers made. Boards dumped.
TRANSPORT TRACK.	- Formation track now completed to S.7.b.98. Track ballasted with chalk to X.19.a.48. Switch track to Bde. H.Q. VILLA WOOD completed. Bridge at corner of BAZENTIN WOOD 50% completed.
VILLA STATION MARTINPUICH.	Completed to R.E. dump MARTINPUICH joining up with existing track there.

HUTTING.	ACID DROP CAMP S.) PIONEER CAMP.) GORDON CAMP.) BDE. H.Q. CAMP,) SHELTER WOOD.)	Equivalent of 10 huts erected. ---- G.OC's hut 50% completed.
	SCOTS REDOUBT CAMP N.	Marked out.
	DIV'L H.Q.	Work on "G" Office and "Q" office extension & on motor garage.
	PLATFORM & ROAD AT VILLA STN.	Work continued.
	DIV'L BATHS.	55% completed.
R.E.DUMP.	Work on road & tramway continued.	

16-11-16.

Major R.E.
for C.R.E., 48th Division.

48th DIVISION.

PROGRESS REPORT FOR 24 HOURS ENDING NOON 15-11-16.

R.E. HEAD QUARTERS
No. 140711
15 NOV 1916
48th DIVISION.

WILLIAM ALLEY.   150 yds. completed ready for trenchboards.
(M.22.c.00 to
M.22.c.43.)

GILBERT ALLEY.   Firebays made in both sides of trench between BAPAUME ROAD and O.G.1.

BOMB STORE.   Nearing completion.
(M.21.d.96.)

DUGOUTS in O.G.1.   Work continued.

SUNKEN ROAD-LE SARS.   Dugouts continued.

WORK IN MARTINPUICH.   7 loads materials collected.

FORWARD TRAMWAY.   125 yds. of sleepers laid.

TRENCHBOARD TRACKS:

    MARTINPUICH-EAUCOURT.   475 ft. of boards made.
                                  72 ft. of track pegged.
                                  Bridge erected alongside WILLIAM ALLEY.

    GILBERT ALLEY.   1000 pegs made.
                                  266 trenchboards collected at M.20.d.67.

    TRANSPORT TRACK.   250 yds. formation prepared.
                                  300 yds. from X.17.b.93 ballasted with chalk.
                                  Wire fence now completed from X.17.b.93. to S.7.b.97.
                                  Bridge over O.G.2. completed.
                                  193 yds. switch to VILLA WOOD Bde. H.Q. completed.

    VILLA STATION,   302 yds. of board laid.
        MARTINPUICH.

HUTTING.   Acid Drop Camp. S.)
          Pioneer Camp.   ) Equivalent of 12 huts completed.
          Gordon Camp.   )

          Platform for tanks. Completed.
          S.1.b.88.

          Div. Hd. Qrs.   No. 1. Mess ready for occupation except for a few small details.

                                Motor garage - Work proceeding.

          Div. Baths.   50% completed.

R.E. DUMP.   Work on road & tramway continued.

15.11.16.

                                  Major R.E.
                                  for C.R.E. 48th Div.

48th DIVISION.

PROGRESS REPORT FOR 24 HOURS ENDING noon 14.11.16.

WILLIAM ALLEY. (M.27.b.88. to M.27.b.99.)	50 men worked on trench commenced on previous night. *100 men lost their way*
GILBERT ALLEY.	Work on putting in firebays along trench forward from BAPAUME Road.
BOMB STORE. (M.21.d.86.)	Commenced excavation.
DUGOUTS in O.G.1.	Work proceeding.
SUNKEN ROAD-LE SARS.	Materials carried and work on cleaning tunnels. Repairing old German dugouts and driving new shafts.
WORK IN MARTINPUICH.	Road through village. - 120 yds. completed. 6 loads materials collected.
FORWARD TRAMWAY.	180 yds. sleepers laid.

TRENCHBOARD TRACKS.

MARTINPUICH-EAUCOURT.	210 yds. trenchboards made & dumped.
GILBERT ALLEY.	39 boards and 400 pegs made and materials carried.
TRANSPORT TRACK.	400 yds. track formation completed from X.17.b.93. 460 yds. fence completed. Fence head now at S.2.c.46. Bridge over O.G.1. completed. " " O.G.2. commenced.
VILLA STATION, MARTINPUICH.	350 yds. boards laid.

HUTTING.	Acid Drop Camp, S. Pioneer Camp. Gordon Camp.	Equivalent of 10 huts erected.
	Rest hut, VILLA STN.	Completed.
	Siding platform & road, VILLA Station.	Work continued.
	Div. Hd. Qrs.	Work progressing well.
	Div. Baths.	40% completed.
R.E. DUMP.	Work on road and tramlines continued.	

Major R.E.
for C.R.E. 48th D.

48th DIVISION.

PROGRESS REPORT FOR 24 HOURS ENDING NOON 13-11-16.

R.E. HEAD QRS.
No. 1371. R.E.
13 NOV 1916
48th DIVISION.

WILLIAM ALLEY. 140 yards completed.
(M.27.b.88 to
M.27.b.99)   100   "   berm cleared.

GILBERT ALLEY. Trench widened to M.26.a.92.

BOMB STORE IN   10% done.
26th AVENUE.

DUGOUTS IN O.G.1 Material carried to site.

SUNKEN ROAD-LE SARS.   Clearing road, corduroying & tunnelling
                       commenced.

WORK IN MARTINPUICH   Road through village. 115 yards completed,
                       including 10 steps.

                       50 men collecting material.

FORWARD TRAMWAY.   150 yards sleepers laid.

TRENCHBOARD TRACKS.

    MARTINPUICH - EAUCOURT.   Completed to M.27.b.6505.

    GILBERT ALLEY.   "   " M.20.d.66.

    TRANSPORT TRACK.   500 yds. formation prepared continuing
                                          from X.17.b.93.
                                          600 yds. fence completed.
                                          Fencehead now at S.1.d.82.

    VILLA STATION)   460 yds. boards laid.
    MARTINPUICH)

HUTTING.

    ACID DROP CAMP S.)
)   Equivalent of 10 huts erected.
    PIONEER CAMP   )   Work continued on road from
                                          CONTALMAISON to PIONEER CAMP.

    GORDON CAMP.   Wash houses - 35% completed.
                                          Stables   - 50%   "
                                          Outhouse   - Made.

    SIDING,   Platform partly erected & all material
    PLATFORM, & ROAD AT   collected outside.
    VILLA STATION.

    REST HUT - VILLA STATION. - Practically completed.

    PLATFORM FOR WATER)   Partially made at store.
    TANKS at S.2.a.19)

DIV. HD. QRS.   No. 1 mess nearly completed.
                          Motor Garage - Progressing.

DIV. BATHS.   Work continued.

R.E. DUMP.   Corduroying of road & laying of tramline
                          continued.

A.O.Walker.

13-11-16

48th DIVISION.

PROGRESS REPORT FOR 24 HOURS ENDING NOON 12.11.16.

WILLIAM ALLEY. (M.27.b.87 to M.27.b.99.)	240 yds. finished and ready for trenchboards. 56 yds. berm cleared.
GILBERT ALLEY.	Widened to 250 yds. S. side of BAPAUME Road.
BOMB STORE in 26th Avenue,	Commenced - Material mostly carried.
MILL O.P. (M.27.c.38.)	Completed.
DUGOUTS in O.G.1.	Work stopped for lack of carrying party. Tunnelling also delayed from same cause.
WORK IN MARTINPUICH.	Road through village. - 103 yds. completed. 50 yds. more prepared for bricks, and damage by shell fire made good.
FORWARD TRAMWAY.	400 yds. beyond GUNPIT LANE packed and sleepered - footway about 300 yds.

TRENCHBOARD TRACKS.

MARTINPUICH-EAUCOURT.	Completed to M.27.d.26.
GILBERT ALLEY.	" " M.20.d.53.
TRANSPORT TRACK.	700 yds. fence completed. 350 yds. " " but tips not painted. Fence head now at S.7.b.31.
VILLA STATION, MARTINPUICH.	400 yds. of boards laid.

HUTTING.	Acid Drop Camp. S.) Pioneer Camp.) Gordon Camp.)	Pioneers rest day. Infantry employed unloading lorries and repairing road from CONTALMAISON to Pioneer Camp.
	Rest Hut, VILLA STN.	Walls completed.
	Div. Hd. Qrs.	Work on No.1. Mess and Motor Garage progressing.
R.E. DUMP.		Corduroy of road and laying of tramline continued. 2 sections completed and 3 sections partially completed.

12.11.16.

A.O. Walker
Major R.E.
For C.R.E., 48th Division.

48th DIVISION.

PROGRESS REPORT FOR 24 HOURS ENDING NOON 11.11.16.

WILLIAM ALLEY. (M.27.b.74 to M.27.b.87.)	130 yards cleared and made ready for trenchboards. 70 yards berm cleared, sides sloped and drained.
GILBERT ALLEY.) MILL O.P.) DUGOUTS in O.G.1.)	Reports sent off but not received.
WORK IN MARTINPUICH.	R.E. Dump. - Pickets, wire etc. collected. Road through village - 181 yds. bricked. (Complete to M.32.a.71.)
FORWARD TRAMWAY.	100 yds. sleepers carried and laid.

TRENCHBOARD TRACKS.

MARTINPUICH-EAUCOURT.	Completed to M.27.c.26.
GILBERT ALLEY.	Completed to M.20.d.41.
VILLA STATION, MARTINPUICH.	500 yds. boards laid. (Completed to S.1.d.31)
TRANSPORT TRACK. (X.17.b.93 to S.7.b.97.)	400 yds. pickets fixed, also one strand of plain wire and tips of pickets painted white.

HUTTING.	Acid Drop Camp S.	Equivalent of 10 huts erected but two destroyed by shell fire.
	Pioneer Camp.	23 huts under erection: 10 50% completed.
	Gordon Camp.	Work on Mess, Wash houses & stables cont'd.
	Pusher's Camp.	Completed.
	Waiting Shed, VILLA Station.	Walls raised 2 ft.
	Div. Hd. Qrs.	No. 1. Mess hut Cont'd. Motor garage commenced.
	Div. Baths.	Framework of main building up.

R. E. DUMP. Corduroy of road and laying of tramline continued.

A.D.Walker.

Major R.E.
For C.R.E., 48th Division.

11.11.16.

48th DIVISION.

PROGRESS REPORT FOR 24 HOURS ENDING noon 10-11-16

WILLIAM ALLEY
(M.27.b.72 to)
(M.22.d.60   ) — Cleared, sides sloped and drained for 400 yards.

GILBERT ALLEY — 700 yards opened out (200 yds. remain to reach BAPAUME ROAD)

MILL O.P. — Excavation complete, building half done.

DUGOUTS in O.G.1. — Progressing.

WORK IN MARTINPUICH. — R.E.DUMP. Pickets, wire, etc. collected.

Road through village, 102 yds. cleared and bricked.

FORWARD TRAMWAY. — Track widened and drained in M.26.b. 270 yds. packed, 100 yds. footboard laid.

TRENCHBOARD TRACKS.

    MARTINPUICH-EAUCOURT — completed to M.27.c.94.

    GILBERT ALLEY — completed to 30 yds. from BAPAUME ROAD.

    VILLA STATION - MARTINPUICH. — 232 trenchboards transported. Will be laid to-night.

    TRANSPORT TRACK. (X.17.b.93 to) (S.7.b.97) — Whole track roughly pegged out: some flints collected for ballasting.

HUTTING.
- Acid Drop Camp S. — Equivalent of 6 huts erected.
- Pioneer Camp — 7 huts commenced.
- Gordon Camp — Progress made on mess and wash-houses
- Pushers' Camp — One more hut erected (6 up to date)
- Waiting Shed VILLA STATION. — Walls half height.
- Div. H.Q. — No. 1 Mess - in progress.
- Div. Baths. — Building - 5% completed.

R.E.DUMP. — Corduroy of road and laying of tramway continued.

Major R.E.
for C.R.E., 48th Division.

10-11-16.

48th DIVISION.

PROGRESS REPORT FOR 24 HOURS ENDING noon 9 - 11 - 16.

GILBERT ALLEY.   200 yards opened up.

WILLIAM ALLEY.   300 Infantry worked on this.

MILL O.P.   In hand.

WORK IN MARTINPUICH. Bde. Baths - 50% completed.
                      R.A.M.C. Dugout - completed.
                      Road through village - 70 yards brick track laid.
                      R.E.Dump - 12 truck loads materials taken up.

FORWARD TRAMWAY. Line maintained, drained, and packed with sleepers.

TRENCHBOARD TRACKS.

   MARTINPUICH - EAUCOURT - Complete to M.27.c.74 - 210 yards boards laid.

   GILBERT ALLEY   - Complete to M.20.d.96 (except 100 yds. along S. side of BAPAUME ROAD)

   VILLA STATION -   No progress on account of shortage of
   MARTINPUICH.   trenchboards.

R.E.DUMP. - Shed for Infantry working party erected.
             Corduroying road and loading platform in hand.

HUTTING.   - Camp "A" (X.16.d.91) equivalent of 5 huts erected.

   (Note 1 hut destroyed and 1 hut damaged by hostile shelling)

   Camp "D" (X.23.a.47) work continued on stables, and washouses and mess

   Camp "O" (X.23.a.27) laid out, road improved and materials unloaded.

   Pushers' Camp (X.11.d.45) - 1 hut erected.

   Waiting shed - VILLA Station - started to-day.

   Detonating shed, "A" dump - completed.

   Div. H.Q. - No.1 Mess - framework completed.

   Coffee Bar (Peake Wood) - erected.

A.D. Walker
Major R.E.
for C.R.E., 48th Division.

9-11-16.

48th DIVISION.

PROGRESS REPORT FOR 24 HOURS ENDING noon 8 - 11 - 16.

OPENING UP OF GILBERT ALLEY. — Opened up but not thoroughly drained to 200 yds of O.G.1.

WORK IN MARTINPUICH. — West End R.E. Dump in formation.
Dugouts — repairs in progress.
Baths — complete except for floor and sandbagging.
Road through village — 100 yards brick track laid and track prepared.
Elephant hut for Police control at M.31.d.91 constructed.

FORWARD TRAMWAY. — 500 yards track cleaned and drained, line repaired where damaged by shells.

TRENCHBOARD TRACKS.

    MARTINPUICH - EAUCOURT - 207 yards boards made and laid.

    GILBERT ALLEY - 79 boards laid completing track to 100 yards S. of where GILBERT ALLEY crosses BAPAUME ROAD.

    VILLA STATION - MARTINPUICH - 350 yards laid up X.6.c.51.

R.E. DUMP. at X.16.a.75 - ground cleared and corduroying road commenced: workshop shed and office completed.

HUTTING. Camp "A" — Equivalent of 3 huts erected.

    Camp "D" — Drying shed completed, stables and mess progressing.

    Pushing party Camp. — 2 more huts erected.

    Detonating Shed at "A" Dump — started.

    Div. H.Q. — Work continuing, 2 more bays for stables started.

ROADS. See separate report submitted to "Q".

Major R.E.
for C.R.E., 48th Division.

8-11-16.

48th DIVISION.

PROGRESS REPORT FOR 24 HOURS ENDING noon 7-11-16.

WORK IN MARTINPUICH. Forward R.E.Dumps formed as under:-

M.16.c.5.1. - Present stock 5200 sandbags, 112 shovels, 200 picks, 40 coils barbed wire & 30 screw posts.

M.15.b.5.2. - Present stock 1000 sandbags, 25 coils barbed wire, 20 screw posts, 12 coils expanding barbed wire.

OPENING UP GILBERT ALLEY.

From crossing of O.G., forward trench is cleared and widened except for 100 yards across valley at 15.b.5.4.

BATHS AT M.33.a.0.6.

Roofing completed, sandbagging walls proceeding.

DUGOUTS.
Repairs in progress.

ROAD THROUGH VILLAGE.

80 yards repaired, 55 yards bricks laid.

FORWARD TRAMWAY.

GUNPIT ROAD to DESTREMONT - as far as ridge the line is sleepered and packed. 100 yards has been widened, graded and sumped.

TRENCHBOARD TRACKS.

MARTINPUICH - EAUCOURT, 150 yards made and laid, total to date 550 yds. up to M.27.c.8.3.

GILBERT ALLEY - 34 trenchboards made; completed to 150 yards of BAPAUME ROAD (about M.26.b.5.8.)

VILLA STATION - MARTINPUICH - 250 yards laid X.11.b.7.6.- X.12.a.1.9.

R.E.DUMP.
All earth removed, cutting made and is now ready for corduroy, all shell holes filled in, Decauville track collected at dump. Carpenters' shed and office erected.

HUTTING.
Camp "A" - equivalent of 6 huts erected.

Camp "D" - Stables, drying room, and officers' mess under construction: roads in camp improved, also road from CONTALMAISON to Camp.

Huts for pushing parties near VILLA STATION:-

1 erected, 3 dismantled.

Div. H.Q. - No.1 mess started.
Div. Baths - Site levelled.
Div. Canteen - completed.

ROADS.
See separate report submitted to "Q".

Major R.E.
for C.R.E., 48th Division

7-11-16.

48th DIVISION.

PROGRESS REPORT FOR 24 HOURS ENDING noon 6-11-16.

WORK IN MARTINPUICH.

1st Field Coy's report not received, but same items as in yesterday's report are in progress.

Village road work carried on from S.W. entrance to village to X roads in main street, mud cleared shell holes filled, sumps constructed.

TRENCHBOARD TRACKS.

GILBERT ALLEY. 44 boards made.

MARTINPUICH - EAUCOURT Track.

155 yards boards made and laid.
Boards now reach M.32.b.6.3.
Track cleared to M.27.c.5.2.

R.E. DUMP.

Filling in of shell holes, and excavation for lorry siding in progress: tramway formation and store hut completed.

HUTTING.

(1) Huts for pushing parties near Villa Station - 1 erected.

(2) "A" Camp. X.16.d.9.1.

Nissen huts completed to date - 4
   do.   do. without linings - 1
In process of erection:-
      75% completed - 5
      25%   do. - 5
less than 25% do. - 8

(3) "D" Camp X.23.a.4.7.

Work continued on drying room, stable road, Officers' Mess.

(4) Div. H.Q. One hut completed with furniture, etc.

(5) Div. Baths in progress.

ROADS. See separate report.

A.D. Walker.

7-11-16.

Major R.E.,
for C.R.E., 48th Division.

48th DIVISION.

PROGRESS REPORT FOR 24 HOURS ENDING noon 5.11.16.

WORK IN MARTINPUICH.

Dugouts in O.G.1.
Dugouts in village.
Bath house for Right Brigade } *Progressing*
R.A.M.C. dugout repairs.

German R.E. stores collected

Road through village: 150 yards worked on, sumps dug, holes filled and surface cleaned.

200 yds trench dug by night

TRENCHBOARD TRACKS.

GILBERT ALLEY.   32 boards made, 170 yards laid, 230 yds fixed.
250 yards GILBERT ALLEY widened and deepened.
Trenchboards now extend to within 50 yards of where GILBERT ALLEY crosses BAPAUME ROAD.

MARTINPUICH-EAUCOURT L'ABBAYE.

136 yards boards made.
109 yards laid.

TRAMWAY.

Cutting on N.E. side of GUNPIT ROAD X.25.d.9.1. widened and deepened from point 8 yds. from road for distance of 43 yds.. Cutting has now a clearance of 4½' each side of rail.

160 yards of track S. of BAPAUME ROAD widened, graded and packed.

HUTTING.

"A" Camp. X.16.d.9.1. - 20 lorry loads NISSEN huts received; four unloading ramps constructed: road near camp repaired and improved.

Div. Baths. X.16.a. - Site cleared and levelled.

Div. H.Q.   One hut practically completed, others under construction.

Roads   see separate report.

W Walker
Maj for
CRE 48th Div
6/11/16

48th DIVISION.
****

> R.E. HEAD QU...
> No. 1187 RE
> 4 NOV 1916
> 48th. DIVISION.

PROGRESS REPORT FOR 24 HOURS ENDING Noon 4.11.16.
* *

WORK IN MARTINPUICH.

    Dugouts in O.G.1. continued.
    Dugouts in village being repaired.
    Bath house near Right Brigade.)
    R.A.M.C. dugout repairs.   ) Progressing
    Collection of material in dump. Progressing.
    Prospecting for wells.   Continuing.
    Trench board track along railway towards VILLA - Cont'd.
    Road through village. Cleaning, draining, and filling shell holes over 150 yards of road.

TRENCHBOARD TRACKS. Gunpit Road to Gilbert Alley. 29 trenchboards made and laid.

    Martinpuich - Eaucourt L'Abbaye. 21 trenchboards made and laid.

TRAMLINE. Platelaying continued. Present railhead M.21.c.3.7. Cutting near Gunpit Road widened. Two breaks in line repaired.

ROADS. Martinpuich - Bazentin and Contalmaison Villa roads maintained.

HUTTING. "A" Camp. (X.16.d.9.1.)
    Nissen huts completed to date - NIL.
     "   " in progress of erection:-
            90% completed 1.
            75%   "   4.
            50%   "   3.
            25%   "   2.
    under 25%   "   8.
                 Total. 18.

(Huts reported 90% completed are those in which only the inner lining remains to be done.)

"D" Camp. (X.23.a.4.7.)

    Work continued on:- Stables.
                        Wash houses.
                        Drying room.
                        Extension to officers mess.
                        Roads in camp.

"C" Camp. (X.23.a.2.7.)
    Site cleared and wired off.

Div. Baths. Work continued.

A S Walker

Major R.E.
4.11.16.   For C.R.E., 48th Divn.

R.E. HEAD QUARTERS
No 1167 R.E.
4 NOV 1916
48th DIVISION

48th DIVISION.

PROGRESS REPORT for 24 hours ending noon 3.11.16.

FRONT AREA.

Dugouts in MARTINPUICH. Work continued.

MARTINPUICH Bath House. Work progressing.

TRACKS. Track from GUNPIT ROAD along GILBERT ALLEY; 1000 yards trenchboards fitted of which 300 yards fixed; 20 new trenchboards made and laid.

Track from MARTINPUICH towards EAUCOURT L'ABBAYE 500 yards track prepared; 38 yards trenchboards made and laid.

MARTINPUICH road from water point to village: 9 sumps dug, mud cleared from road, material collected for filling holes.

ROADS. CONTALMAISON-MARTINPUICH. Continued digging sumps, cleaning roads and laying bricks.

BAZENTIN-MARTINPUICH. Continued clearing for laying corduroy; 25 logs laid.

General maintenance carried out.

TRAMLINES. Rails dumped at GUNPIT ROAD, VILLA STATION and CENTRE WOOD.
Track laid up to M.21.c.2.6.; head of formation 500 yards further on.

150 yards rough planking laid and tramway line where damaged by shell fire made good.

CAMPS. Div. Hd. Qrs. 2 more huts under construction.

Camp "A". Construction of NISSEN huts continued; 5 more huts commenced; 3 huts floored; frames of 5 huts completed and outer shell of 3 huts not quite completed.

Div. Baths, CONTALMAISON. Work in progress.

4.11.16.

Major R.E.
For C.R.E., 48th Division.

Vol 21

CONFIDENTIAL.

WAR DIARY.

of

48th (South Midland) Divisional Engineers.

From 1st December 1916.........to........31st December 1916.

(Volume 22)

Army Form C. 2118.

WAR DIARY
or
INTELLIGENCE SUMMARY.

(Erase heading not required.)

Instructions regarding War Diaries and Intelligence Summaries are contained in F. S. Regs., Part II. and the Staff Manual respectively. Title pages will be prepared in manuscript.

Place	Date 1916.	Hour	Summary of Events and Information	Remarks and references to Appendices
LOZENGE WOOD, FRICOURT.	Decr. 1-15		See attached Daily Progress Reports	
	15		1/1st Field Coy. moved to SHELTER WOOD.	
			1/2nd Field Coy. moved to BAZENTIN - le - PETIT.	
	16		15th Division relieved 48th Division. R.E. Headquarters moved to ALBERT. 1/1st Field Coy. remained under orders of C.R.E., 15th Division. 1/2nd " " " " " " " 2/1st " " " " " C.E. IIIrd Corps.	
ALBERT	16th-31st		At ALBERT.	

Major R.E.
for C.R.E. 48th Div.

1908 R.E

48th DIVISION.

PROGRESS REPORT FOR 24 HOURS ENDING NOON 15.12.16.

DUGOUTS.

MIDDLE CUTTING (W. of MARTINPUICH-BUTTE ROAD)

No. 4. Right lateral.	Started and advanced to 7'6".	
No. 5. O.G.Entrance.	Sunk to an inclined distance of	33'
No. 6. do.	do.	26'

LE SARS CUTTING.

No. 2. Left lateral.	Advanced a total of	12'9".
No. 3. Right "	do.	12'6".

A certain amount of surface work had to be done securing Entrances.

WIRING SUPPORT LINE.   40 yds. wired near M.22.b.55.

TRAMWAY. Cutting Road to Acid Drop Copse.

500 yds. laid to date, of which 400 yds. ballasted and 450 yds. boarded.

WATER SUPPLY TO ACID DROP COPSE. Practically completed and ready for use.

HUTTING.

Shelter Wood S. - 3 Amiens huts worked on.

15th D.A.C. Camp.- 14 huts completed. 1 under construction.

Div. Train Lines. -Huts completed 4.
W.29.b.59.   Huts under erection 1.

48th R.A. wagon Lines. -   12 huts under erection.
X.22.a.

TRUCKS FOR AMBULANCE. - 6 up to date finished (Work completed)

[signature]

Major R.E.
For C.R.E., 48th Division.

15.12.16.

1897 RE

48th DIVISION.

PROGRESS REPORT FOR 24 HOURS ENDING NOON 14.12.16.

GILBERT ALLEY.   Trenchboarded up to M.15.b.43. (80 trenchboards)

WILLIAM ALLEY.   Trenchboard track raised in places, in other places placed outside trench.

CRESCENT ALLEY. Falls of earth cleared: materials for revetting collected.

DUGOUTS.

  MIDDLE CUTTING (West of MARTINPUICH-BUTTE Road.)

    No. 4. Entrance.   Opening out at bottom, sufficient head-cover (22-23 ft.) having been obtained.

    No. 5. Entrance.   Timbering and securing entrance, etc. which had been knocked about.

  LE SARS CUTTING.

    No. 1. Left Lateral.   Total length.   36'0".
    No. 2. Right   "   "   "   16'0".
    No. 3. Left   "   "   "   5'0".

Nos. 1. and 2. have been connected up and the Infantry are already making use of same for shelter.

Great scarcity of timber due to carrying party again failing.

WIRING SUPPORT LINE.   100 yds. wired near M.22.a.33.

TRAMWAY TO ACID DROP COPSE.   200 yds. tramway laid (290 yds. to date.) 300 yds. formation prepared.

HUTTING. Div. Hd. Qrs.   Incinerator - Completed.
                  Drying Shed.- Walls completed and roof begun.

    15th D.A.C. Lines.)   Huts completed.   13.
      X.15.c.   )   Huts under erection.   2.

    Div. Train Lines.)   Huts completed.   3.
      W.29.b.59.   )   Huts under erection.   1.

    Div. Bath House.)   Clarifying tanks: 1" pipe connected
      X.17.b.41.   )   to tanks and all work completed.

    Camp W. of MARTINPUICH.   Work continued.

48th DIVISION.

PROGRESS REPORT FOR 24 HOURS ENDING NOON 13.12.16.

GILBERT ALLEY.   50 trenchboards and 20 revetting frames carried.

WILLIAM ALLEY.   Falls of earth cleared.

CRESCENT ALLEY.   No work as party was employed in carrying.

DUGOUTS.

    MIDDLE CUTTING (W. of MARTINPUICH.)

        No. 4. O.G. entrance.   Total depth   35'6".
        No. 5. O.G.   "   "   "   27'6".
        No. 6. O.G.   "   "   "   25'0".

    LE SARS CUTTING.

        No. 1. Left lateral.   Total length   33'6".
        No. 2. Right   "   "   "   10'2".
        No. 3.   "   "   "   "   7'3".

    BRIGADE HD.QRS.

    Dugout extension completed.

FORWARD R.E. DUMP.   Formed at M.17.c.17.

WIRE TRACK.   Laid from M.16.d.61 to M.16.d.86.

TRACK S.1.b.53 to BAPAUME Road at R.36.a.54.   Posts put in at 20 yards interval along track.

TRAMWAY. to ACID DROP COPSE.   175 yds. formation made.
                                        90 yds. tramway laid.

HUTTING.

    Div. Hd. Qrs. - Incinerator.) 75% completed.
                Drying Shed.)

    15th D.A.C. Lines.   - Completed to date, 12 huts.
      X.15.c.   Under construction, 3 "

    Div. Train Lines.   - 2 huts completed, 2 under construction.
      W.29.b.59.

    Div. Bath House.   - Clarifying tanks: pipes for tanks cut
      X.17.b.41.   and threaded ready for use.

48th DIVISION.

1863 R.E.

PROGRESS REPORT FOR 24 HOURS ENDING NOON 12.12.16.

GILBERT ALLEY.   Trenchboarded up to M.15.b.42.
Sumps dug: cleaning and baling done.

WILLIAM ALLEY.   Company of Pioneers clearing out falls of earth, scooping out water, and cutting and painting white guide posts.

CRESCENT ALLEY.   5 yds. more revetted.

DUGOUTS.

  MIDDLE CUTTING (West of MARTINPUICH-BUTTE Road.)

  No. 4. O.G. entrance.   Sunk to an inclined depth of 35'.
  No. 5.   do.   do.   26'.
  No. 6.   do.   do.   15'.

  LE SARS CUTTING (New British dugouts.)

  No. 1. Left lateral.   Total length from stairway   23'9".
  No. 1. Right   "   do.   3'0".
  No. 2. entrance.   Landing at bottom advanced to 4'6".
  No. 2. Right lateral. Advanced to total of   3'9".
  No. 3. entrance.   Landing at bottom advanced to 4'0".
  No. 3. Right lateral. Advanced to total of   4'0".

WIRING FRONT LINE.   160 men wired from M.16.b.33 South and joined previous work.

SANDBAGGING TANKS, M.28.a.14. - 50% completed.

TRACK S.1.b.53 to BAPAUME ROAD at R.36.a.54.   Intermediate pickets taken to site.

TRAMWAY.   Materials for CRESCENT ALLEY-DEAD MULE CORNER taken to CRESCENT ALLEY.
Materials for Div. Bath-Gordon Camp line taken to Div. Baths.

HUTTING.

  Div. Hd. Qrs.   Drying shed - Panels prepared.

  15th D.A.C. lines. - Equivalent of one Nissen hut erected.

  Div. Train Lines. - One hut completed, 2 under erection.
  W.29.b.59.

  Old Canadian Camp W. of MARTINPUICH. - Work continued.

  Div. Bath house.   - Clarifying tanks: laying of box drains and
  X.17.b.41.   revetting of walls completed.

WATER SUPPLY TO ACID DROP S. 240' pipe laid. Tanks erected.
and GORDON CAMPS.

Major R.E.
for C R E 48th Div.

48th DIVISION.   1845 R.E.

PROGRESS REPORT FOR 24 HOURS ENDING NOON 11.12.16.

GILBERT ALLEY.   30 cu. yds. dug in sump.
                      Trenchboarded up to M.15.d.1095.

WILLIAM ALLEY.   Pegging down trenchboards which now extend to
                      Sunken Road, Le Sars.

CRESCENT ALLEY.   15 yds. revetted. (To date 35 yds.)

DUGOUTS.

    Brigade -   4 frames fixed.

    Le Sars Cutting - 3 new entrances to old German dugouts
                      under construction: present depths

                            No. 1.   25'9".
                            No. 2.   37'0".
                            No. 3.   42'0". and horizontal
                                     approaches being made.

    Middle Cutting - M.22.b.38.   6 old German entrances exist

                      as under:-

                            No. 1.   Smashed in.
                            No. 2.   Cleared for distance of 8' beyond
                                     which it will not be taken.
                            No. 3.) Cleared and re-timbered: dugout
                              &)   connection between these two but
                            No. 4.) only 8' of cover.
                            No. 4.   continues to a depth of 30' on the
                                     incline.
                            No. 5.   Entrance cleared and re-timbered:
                                     depth 22' on the incline.
                            No. 6.   Entrance cleared and re-timbered:
                                     depth to 14' on the incline.

    Eaucourt L'Abbaye Cutting - M.22.b.77.   German dugout opened
                      out - chamber 10' x 8' in good condition.

    Causeway - M.22.b.58. - Entrance to German dugout 10' x 8'
                      cleared.

                      Dugout 50 yds. North of the above 10' x 8'
                      entrance cleared.

WIRE TRACK.   270 yds. laid: terminus now 60 yds. short of road

              near TAIL.

HIGH STREET, MARTINPUICH.   Cleared and repaired M.32.c.48 to
                                                M.32.a.31.

                                                        P.T.O.

HUTTING.

    Div. Hd. Qrs. - Drying Shed.)   Continued.
                   Incinerator.)

    Canadian Camp W. of MARTINPUICH - Work Continued.

    Nissen huts for 15th D.A.C.   -   do.

    Nissen huts for Gas School.   - 2 completed.

    R.A. Camp - X.16.d.19 -   Material unloaded but final site not settled.

    Div. Train Camp.   2 nissen huts under erection

AMBULANCE TRAMWAY TRUCKS. - 2 more trucks completed.

WATER SUPPLY TO ACID DROP S. 300 ft. pipe laid. Frames for
and GORDON CAMPS.   supporting tanks made ready for erection.

DIVL BATHS CLARIFYING TANKS. Excavation completed.
    X.17.b.41.   Revetting 80% completed.
                             Terracing of end completed.

11.12.16.

                                        Major R.E.
                             For C.R.E., 48th Division.

48th DIVISION.

PROGRESS REPORT FOR 24 HOURS ENDING NOON 10.12.16.

GILBERT ALLEY.   Cleaned and trenchboards straightened for 700 yards from BAPAUME Road.
Trenchboards now reach M.15.c.88.

WILLIAM ALLEY.   Trenchboard track completed up to SUNKEN ROAD, LE SARS, M.16.c.4810.

CRESCENT ALLEY.   10 yards revetted and 12 frames put in.

DUGOUTS.

    LE SARS CUTTING.   Of the three new dugout entrances, two have been continued on the incline one to 36 ft. the other to 41 ft., the third has reached its full depth and has been turned for a length of 22 ft.

Repairs to German dugouts carried out at following places

(map references not known):-

(1) EAUCOURT L'ABBAYE CUTTING East of MARTINPUICH-BUTTE Road - Entrance being opened out.

(2) CAUSEWAY across MARTINPUICH-BUTTE Road - entrance cleared.

(3) DUGOUT 20 yards N. of (2) - Entrance cleared.

(4) CUTTING directly W. of MARTINPUICH-BUTTE Road - Six entrances to dugout cleared.

BRIGADES - 4 frames fixed.

TRENCHBOARD TRACK.

    Infantry track to BAPAUME Road.) Track pegged out with
    S.1.b.53 to R.36.a.54.   ) pickets.

HUTTING.

    Div. Hd. Qrs. - Drying shed.   Continued.
                   Incinerator.   Commenced.
                   Motor garage. Covering in of back completed.

Canadian Camp, W.) Work continued.
of MARTINPUICH.   )

Nissen huts for) Completed.   11.
15th D.A.C.   ) Under construction.   2.

Ablution bench.   ) Completed.
CONTALMAISON Chateau.)

P. T. O.

HUTTING, Cont'd.

    R.A. Camp.) Material unloaded and carried.
n   X.16.d.19.)

AMBULANCE TRAMWAY TRUCKS.   Two trucks covered with canvas and two
                                        fitted with framework.

WATER SUPPLY to ACID DROP S.)140 ft. pipe laid. Pipe connected to
& GORDON CAMPS   )main and two cocks put in.

                                                                    A.S. Walker

                                                                   Major R.E.
10th Dec. 1916.   For C.R.E., 48th Division.

48th DIVISION.

PROGRESS REPORT FOR 24 HOURS ENDING NOON 9-12-16.

GILBERT ALLEY. — Revetting material, including 40 A frames, carried to site.
Trenchboards laid up or along trench to O.G.1.

WILLIAM ALLEY. — Up to date 50 yds. revetted and 50 more yds. prepared for revetment.
Trenchboards laid alongside trench to M.22.a.49.

CRESCENT ALLEY. — 30 revetting frames put in/up to date, starting from M.27.b.92.

DUGOUTS.

    BATTN. H.Q.)
    GILBERT ALLEY.) Report not received.
)
    O.G.1.)

    BRIGADE. — 2 frames fixed.

WATER TANKS AT M.27.d.21. — Protected with sandbags.

TRAMWAYS.

    MIDDLE WOOD SIDING. — Platform made and completed.

TRENCHBOARD TRACK. — Southern track laid from M.28.a.99 approximately parallel to road to causeway at M.22.b.58 and on to M.16.d.61.

HUTTING. DIV. H.Q. — Drying shed — continued.

    SOUP KITCHEN) — Completed.
    M.31.d.84)

    CANADIAN CAMP W.) — work continued.
    of MARTINPUICH.)

    Nissen huts for) — Continued.
    15th T.A.C.)

    GAS SCHOOL. — 2 Nissen huts — 75% completed.

    ABLUTION BENCH — CONTALMAISON CHATEAU — 50% completed.

    DIV. TRAIN CAMP) — Nissen huts erected — 25% — 5
    W.29.b.59.)   "   "   " under 25% — 5

    R.A. Wagon Lines) — Camp taped out and material brought
    Camp. M.16.d.19.) to site.

WATER SUPPLY TO ACID DROP S.) — 20ft of 2" pipe laid.
& GORDON CAMPS.) Site for tanks cleared & prepared.

AMBULANCE TRAMWAY TRUCKS. — Framework for covers to two trucks made.

9-12-16.

Major R.E.
for C.R.E., 48th Division.

1803 R.E

48th DIVISION.

PROGRESS REPORT FOR 24 HOURS ENDING NOON 8 - 12 - 16.

GILBERT ALLEY. - 100 yds prepared for revetment.

WILLIAM ALLEY. - Revetting completed for 50 yds.

CRESCENT ALLEY.- 150 yds prepared for revetting.

DUGOUTS.

    BATTN. H.Q.) - 3 frames fixed.
    GILBERT ALLEY)

    O.G.1. - 4 frames fixed.

    BRIGADE - 4 frames fixed.

R.E.DUMP - MARTINPUICH.- 21 truck loads of stores sent from CONTALMAISON.

TRAMWAYS.

    MIDDLE WOOD SIDING. - Rails laid and level crossing made.

RATION DUMP - GILBERT ALLEY - 25% completed.

HUTTING. SOUP KITCHEN - MARTINPUICH - 75% completed.

    DIV. H.Q. - R.A.Mess hut - Completed.

        Drying Room - Commenced.

    CANADIAN CAMP W.) - Work continued.
    of MARTINPUICH.)

    NISSEN HUTS FOR) - Completed - 9
    15th D.A.C.) 75% "hut - 1

    GAS SCHOOL. - 2 Nissen 30% completed.

    DIV. CANTEEN) - Seats made & fixed, canvas put up round
    A.16.d.86) sides: trenchboard track laid.

WATER SUPPLY TO ACID DROP CAMP. - Trench completed, piping carried to site.

8-12-16.

Major R.E.
for C.R.E., 48th Division.

48th DIVISION.

PROGRESS REPORT FOR 24 HOURS ENDING NOON 7 - 12 - 16.

GILBERT ALLEY. — Cleared and repaired 250 yds. from BAPAUME ROAD.
Trenchboarded up M.15.b. central (30 yds short of Chalk Trench)

WILLIAM ALLEY. — Revetting complete for 15 yds.
Trenchboard to M.22.a.56.

CRESCENT ALLEY. — 260 yds prepared for revetment.

~~DUGOUTS.~~

DUGOUTS {

BATTN. H.Q.   ) — 3 frames fixed.
GILBERT ALLEY)   Material carried & some revetting done.

O.G.1.   — 5 frames fixed.
                     4 "   carried.

LE SARS.   — 20 ft. horizontal gallery timbered.
                     Width narrowed to 3ft.

BRIGADE.   — 12 frames fixed.

RATION DUMPS.

26th AVENUE   — Finished.

GILBERT ALLEY — 25% finished.

TRAMWAYS.

MIDDLE WOOD SIDING — 60 yds formation prepared.
                    Points & 3 lengths rail laid.

HUTTING.   DIV. H.Q. — R.A. Mess — Partitioning & lining.
                                    Cookhouse completed.

Camouflaging Nissen hut) — completed.
X.21.b.central.   )

Canadian Camp W. of)   — reconstruction continued.
MARTINPUICH   )

Scots Redoubt & Shelter) — 250 trenchboards delivered.
Wood Camp.   )

Nissen huts for 15th D.A.C.) — 2 under construction.
X.15.c.   )

Gas School   —   2 huts started.

WATER SUPPLY. To Northern Group) — 130 yds trench dug, 1' wide x
               Nissen hut Camps)   2'6" deep.

7-12-16.

Major R.E.
for C.R.E., 48th Division.

48th DIVISION.

PROGRESS REPORT FOR 24 HOURS ENDING NOON 6-12-16.

GILBERT ALLEY. — Trenchboarded up to M.15.c.51.
Work on sumps. (Note: the work on 2 large sumps is now being discontinued.) ~~as per C.O.'s orders~~.

WILLIAM ALLEY. — Trenchboarded up to M.22.a.64.
Revetting in progress.

DUGOUTS.

BATTN. H.Q.) 3 frames fixed
GILBERT ALLEY) 32 men carrying.

O.G.1. — 4 frames fixed.

LE SARS — Corners of top & bottom shafts turned and now 6ft from bottom of shafts.
40 men carrying.

BRIGADE. — 8 frames fixed.

RATION DUMPS.

26th AVENUE — 60% finished.

GILBERT ALLEY — 20% "

TRAMWAY. — MIDDLE WOOD SIDING — ground prepared.

HUTTING. DIV. H.Q. — R.A. Mess — partitioning and lining.

Camouflaging Nissen hut at X.21.b. central — 50% completed.

Old Canadian Camp W. of MARTINPUICH — accommodation prepared for two platoons.

WATER SUPPLY. — To Northern Group Nissen Hut Camps — started.

A.S. Walker.

6-12-16.

Major R.E.
for C.R.E., 48th Division.

1756 R.E.

48th DIVISION.

PROGRESS REPORT FOR 24 HOURS ENDING NOON 5.12.16.

GILBERT ALLEY.   Cleaned and repaired to Bttn. Hd. Qrs.

WILLIAM ALLEY.   Revetting started. Pioneers start night work tonight.

DUGOUTS.

    Bttn. Hd. Qrs.)   Two frames of horizontal gallery fixed.
    Gilbert Alley.)   50 men carrying cases.

    O.G.1.   Entrance knocked in by shell fire now repaired. One more step added to shaft.

    Le Sars.   100 men carrying material.
    Report on frames not received.

RATION DUMP.)   30% finished.
26th Avenue.)

RATION DUMP.)   10% finished.
Gilbert Avenue.)

HUTTING.

    Div. Hd. Qrs. R.A.Mess. - Lining and putting in partitions. Cookhouse partly erected.

    R.A.M.C. Dugout.)   Repairs completed.
    X.22.a.76.   )

    Nissen hut camps.   Latrines, fencing and drainage continued.

    Div. Soup Kitchen.)   Laid trench board track to
    X.11.b.51.   )   shelters.

    Old Canadian Camp)   Work of reconstruction started.
    W. of Martinpuich.)

5.12.16.

Major R.E.
For C.R.E., 48th Division.

48th DIVISION.

PROGRESS REPORT FOR 24 HOURS ENDING NOON 4 - 12 - 16.

GILBERT ALLEY. - 160 men working on sumps.

DUGOUTS.

    BATTN. H.Q.) - One shaft finished & one practically completed.
    GILBERT ALLEY)   Horizontal gallery started.
                    36 men carrying cases.

    O.G.1.   Both shafts finished & air shaft opened between
                       them.
                       100 men carrying cases.

    LE SARS.   77 cases fixed.

BOMB STORES.

    CRESCENT ALLEY - Finished.

R.E. DUMP-MARTINPUICH. - 3 night trains and 2 day train loads of
                                stores sent from CONTALMAISON.

TRAMWAYS.

    VILLA STATION SIDING. - Completing drain.
                              Siding & road completed except for chalk
                              & ballast.

    VILLA WOOD.   -   200 yds fence along tramline put up.
                              Platform at VILLA WOOD completed.

TRENCHBOARD TRACKS. -

    TO RIGHT SECTOR. - 140 yds boards made.
                            Track completed to M.22.a.01.

    TO LEFT SECTOR - 120 yds boards fixed - 30 boards made.
                          150 pickets cut & fixed.
                          Branch laid from S.2.a.22 to S.2.a.34
                          (BAZENTIN - MARTINPUICH ROAD)

HUTTING. DIV. H.Q. - R.A.Mess - Walls completed. Lining &
                              partitions commenced.

        MOTOR GARAGE - Completed.

        ROAD TO SIGNAL) 20' road completed.
        CAMP.   )

        NISSEN HUT CAMPS. - Latrines, fencing, & drainage continued.

        R.A.M.C. DUGOUT) - Repairs practically completed.
        A.22.a.76   )

        DIV. SOUP KITCHEN) - Shelters completed, seats made &
        X.11.b.51.   )   canvas fixed to sides.

4-12-16.   Major R.E.
                                                     for C.R.E., 48th Division.

48th DIVISION.   1701 R.E.

PROGRESS REPORT FOR 24 HOURS ENDING NOON 3 - 12 - 16.

DUGOUTS.

    BATTN. H.Q.   ) - 52 ft. driven.
    GILBERT ALLEY)

    O.G.1.   - 85% done - 50 men carrying frames to site.

    LE SARS   - 65 ft. driven - 100 men carrying frames to site.

BOMB STORES.

    CRESCENT ALLEY - 90% done.

TRAMWAYS.

    VILLA STATION SIDING. - Tramline laid & practically completed.

    SOUTHERN BRANCH.   - Track laid and completed through from MARTINPUICH Junction to CRESCENT ALLEY M.28.a.24 - Fit for engines up to Bde. Headquarters.

    VILLA WOOD.)
    X.17.b.53.   )   - Completed except for 200 yds of boarding on tramline.
      to   )
    X.12.c.56.   )

TRENCHBOARD TRACK.

    TO RIGHT SECTOR.   - 85 yds boards made. 5 sets of steps cut and revetted in WILLIAM ALLEY. Clearing & sumping of WILLIAM ALLEY carried on - Track laid for 910 yds. in and up WILLIAM ALLEY.

    TO LEFT SECTOR.   - 150 yds track laid & fixed. 20 boards made & boards carried. Track complete as far as BAPAUME ROAD M.26.b.49.

HUTTING.   DIV'L H.Q.   -   R.A.Mess - Putting on roof and walls partly covered.

    R.A.M.C.DUGOUT.) Repairs - 2/3rds completed.
    X.22.d.76   )

    DIV.SOUP KITCHEN) Framework of both shelters completed.
    X.11.b.51.   ) One roof fixed & one partly fixed.

3-12-16.
                                                  Major R.E.
                                    for C.R.E., 48th Division.

1694 R.E.

48th DIVISION.

PROGRESS REPORT FOR 24 HOURS ENDING NOON 2 - 12 - 16.

GILBERT ALLEY. - Digging big sumps - 200 cu. yds. done.

DUGOUTS.

    BATTN. H.Q.   )   47 ft. driven
    GILBERT ALLEY)   50 loads frames carried up.

    O.G.1.   - 78% done.

    LE SARS,   - 60 ft driven.   100 loads frames carried up.

BOMB STORES.

    CRESCENT ALLEY - 80% done.

R.E. DUMP - MARTINPUICH. - 12 trucks stores sent from CONTALMAISON.

TRAMWAYS.

    VILLA STATION SIDINGS - Laying Railway line.

    SOUTHERN BRANCH   - 80 yds track completed.
                              208 yds track laid and ready for use.
                              203 yds rail placed in position.
                              To complete this track to CRESCENT ALLEY,
                              580 yds track laying and 780 yds linking
                              still required.

    VILLA WOOD.   - 16 yds rails laid - 50 yds ballasted.

    WAGON SIDING)   - Metalling laid on fascines.
    X.17.b.53.   )   Steps made from road.

TRENCHBOARD TRACKS.

    TO RIGHT SECTOR.   - Completed through from MAMETZ WOOD, X.17.b.53
                              to M.27.b.72 from which point 404 yds boards
                              are laid in trench thence 330 yds laid on
                              berm, 160 yds laid as track on left side, then
                              420 yds in trench.

    TO LEFT SECTOR.   - 39 Trenchboards made laid and fixed: gap
                              between GUNPIT LANE and BAPAUME ROAD reduced
                              by 75 yds.

HUTTING.

    DIV. H.Q.   - R.A. MESS - Completing frame.

                   MOTOR GARAGE - Shedding completed.
                                   40' road laid.

    NISSEN HUTS CAMPS.   - Fencing & latrines in hand.

    R.A.M.C. DUGOUT)   - Revetting big fall of earth.
    X.22.a.76   )

    STAGE FOR CURIOS)   - Completed.
    X.21.b.80   )

R.E. DUMP.   -   8700 feet of wire netting pathway completed.

2-12-16.

                                                  Major R.E.
                                                for C.R.E. 48th Div

48th DIVISION.

PROGRESS REPORT FOR 24 HOURS ENDING NOON 1-12-16.

GILBERT ALLEY. - Digging big sump - 200 cubic yards done.

DUGOUTS.

    BATTN. H.Q.   ) - 42ft driven.
    GILBERT ALLEY.)

    O.G.1.   - 75% done.

    LE SARS.   - 53ft driven.

BOMB STORES.   - CRESCENT ALLEY - 75% done.

O.P. at S.2.b.9.4. - 30% done.

TRAMWAYS.

    VILLA STATION SIDING   - Making up permanent way & draining. Drawing rails to complete.

    SOUTHERN BRANCH   - To complete this branch to CRESCENT ALLEY 700 yds track laying & 800yds linking up is still required. Earthwork nearly finished.

    VILLA WOOD   - 90 yds rail laid - 150 yds ballasted.

    WAGON SIDING)   - 26ft fascines roadway made.
    X.17.b.53.   )

TRENCHBOARD TRACKS.

    MARTINPUICH - EAUCOURT - 100 yds boards made.
                                         80 yds boards laid in WILLIAM ALLEY.
                                         60 yds track carried.
                                     Track complete to M.27.b.72.

    TO LEFT SECTOR   - 35 boards made.
                                    100 yds track laid & 200 yds track fixed. The gap between BAPAUME ROAD and R.E. DUMP MARTINPUICH has been filled with the exception of about 150 yds.

    INFANTRY TRACK.   - 280 yds laid - Track joined up at N. end with CONTALMAISON VILLA - MARTINPUICH Track - 130 yds track laid from O.G.1. back towards VILLA WOOD.

HUTTING.   DIV'L H.Q.   - R.A.Mess - Joists & frames for walls erected & floor partly laid.

               MOTOR GARAGE   - 20ft road laid. Putting on roof to shedding & laying chalk.

    NISSEN HUT CAMPS.   - Drainage, fencing and latrines in hand.

    R.A.M.C. DUGOUT)   - Repairing.
    X.22.a.76   )
STAGE FOR DIV. CURIOS.   - 60% finished.

R.E.DUMP.   Trench pathway of   ) 1800' completed.
            wire netting & stakes) Total to date 6,900.

                                                                                 Major R.E.
                                                           for C.R.E., 48th Division.

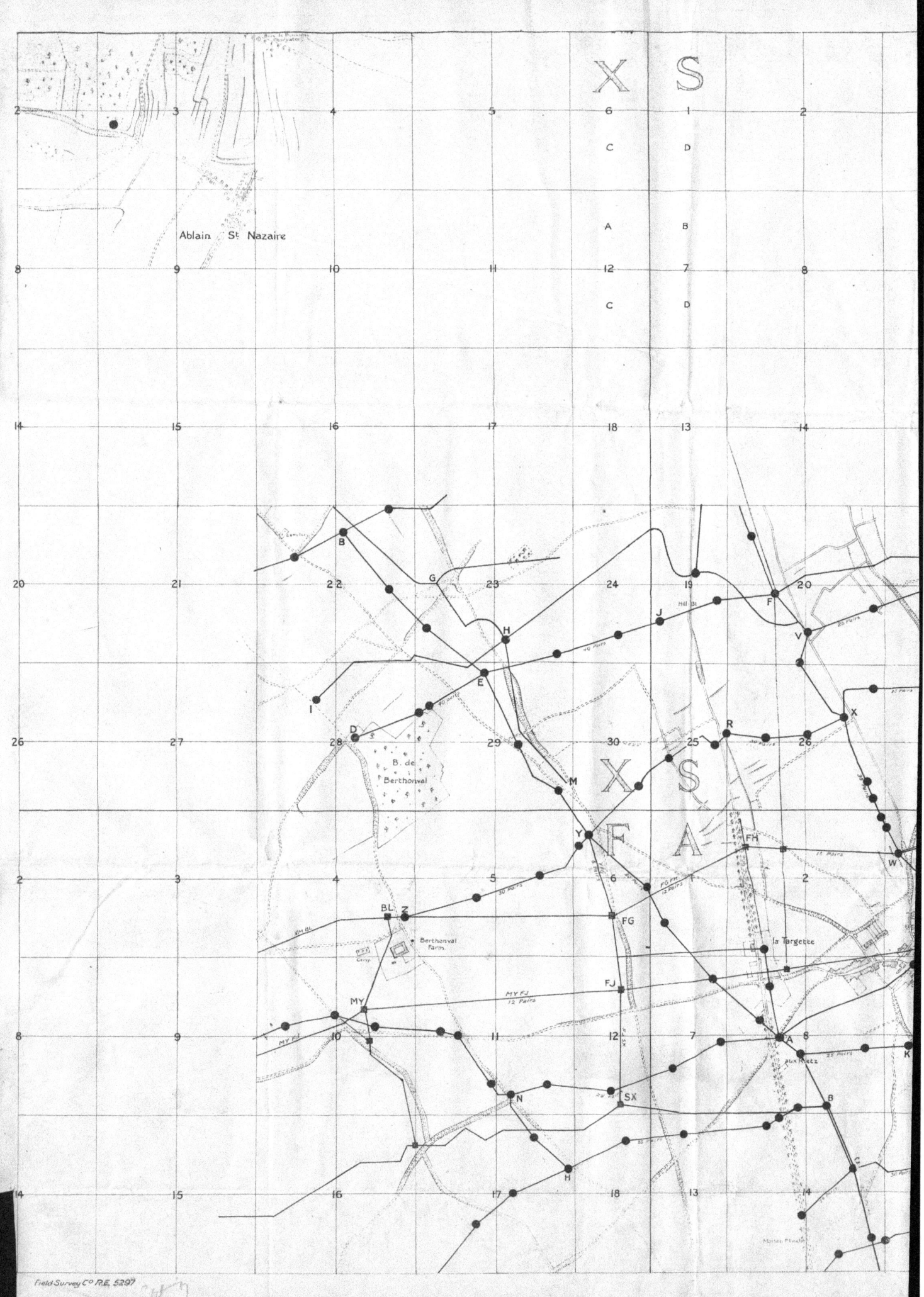

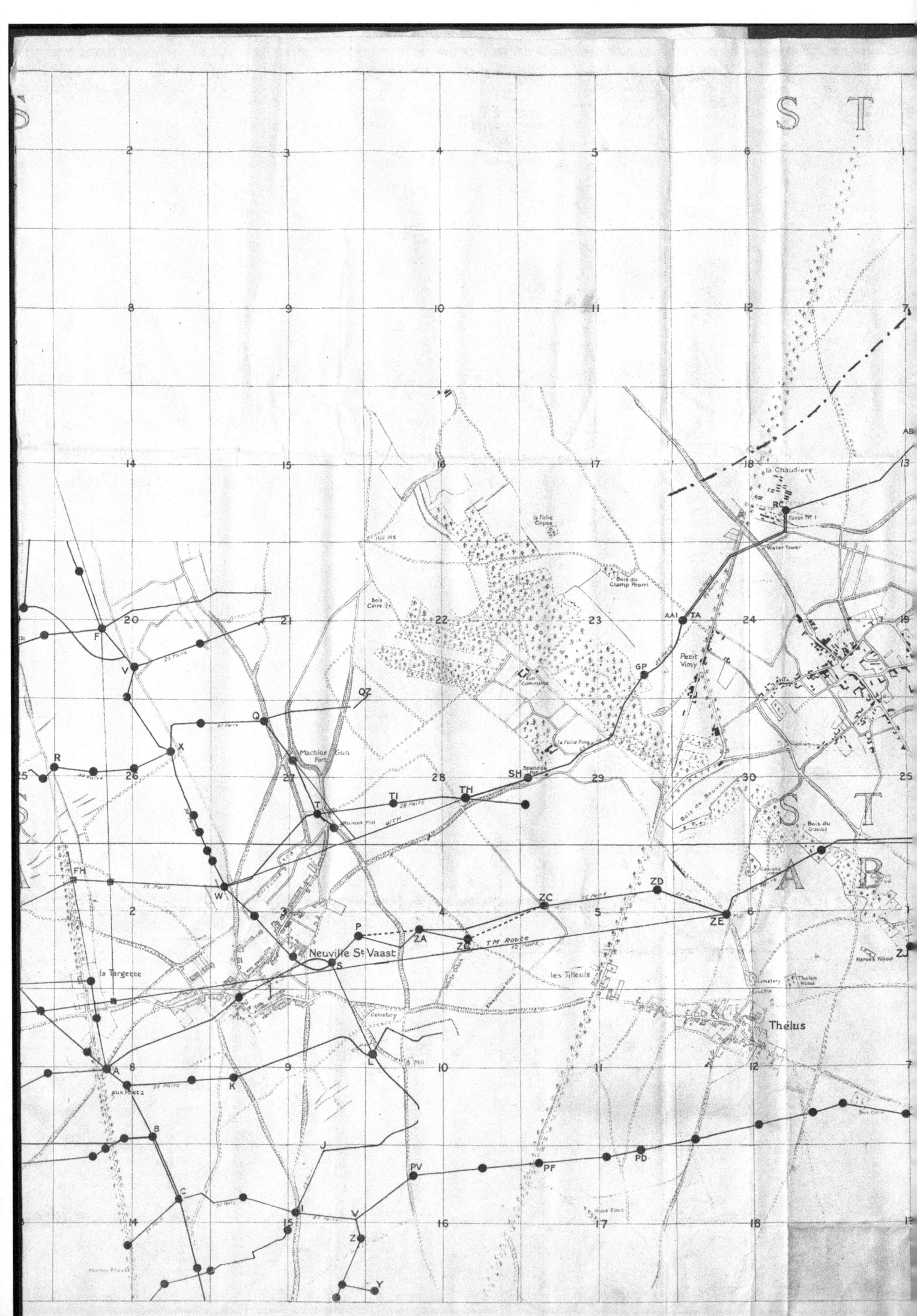

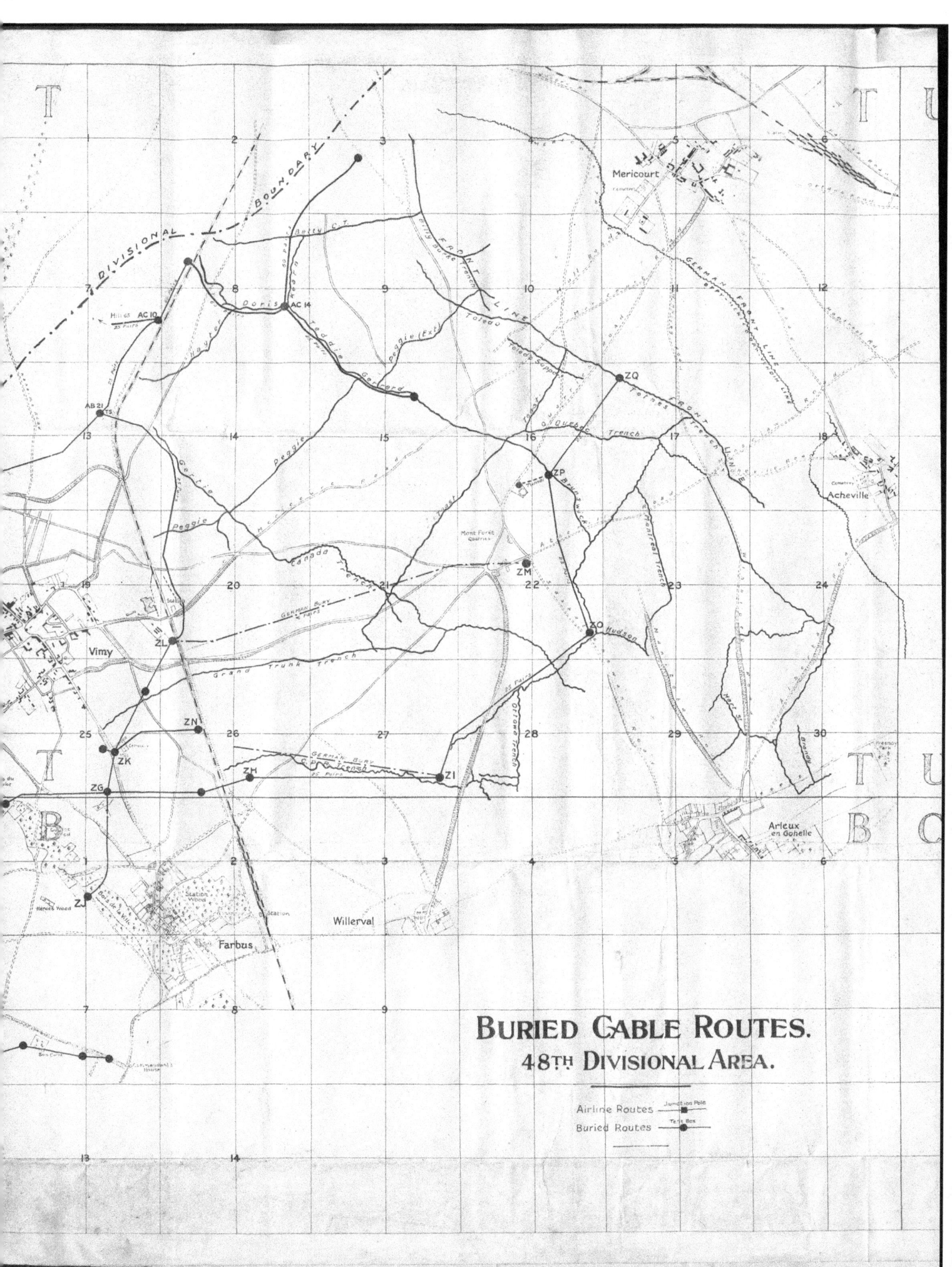

BURIED CABLE ROUTES.
48TH DIVISIONAL AREA.

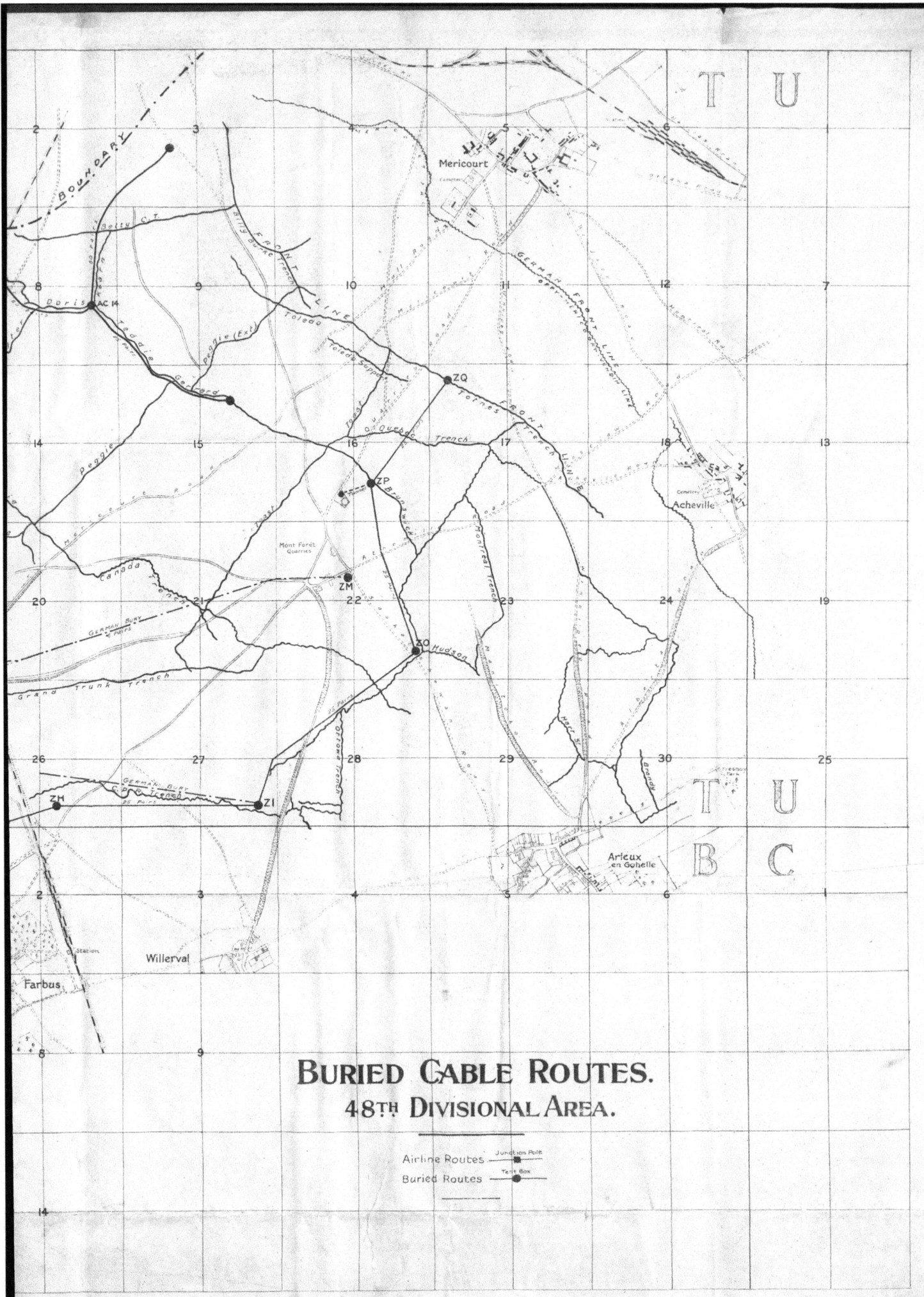

BURIED CABLE ROUTES.
48TH DIVISIONAL AREA.

Vol 22

CONFIDENTIAL.

WAR DIARY

of

48th (South Midland) Divisional Engineers.

From 1st January 1917.........to..........31st January 1917.

(Volume 23)

Army Form C. 2118.

WAR DIARY
or
INTELLIGENCE SUMMARY.

(Erase heading not required.)

Instructions regarding War Diaries and Intelligence Summaries are contained in F. S. Regs., Part II. and the Staff Manual respectively. Title pages will be prepared in manuscript.

Place	Date 1917	Hour	Summary of Events and Information	Remarks and references to Appendices
ALBERT.	Jan. 1		Moved to BAIZIEUX. (Rest Area.)	
	2		A/C.R.E. attended Divisional Conference.	
BAIZIEUX.	3		At BAIZIEUX A/C.R.E. Routine A/Adjutant "	
	4		ditto.	
	5		At BAIZIEUX. A/C.R.E. attended Divisional Conference. A/Adjutant - Routine.	
	6		At BAIZIEUX. A/C.R.E. - Routine. A/Adjutant - "	
	7		ditto.	
	8		ditto. Division moved to Back Training Area.	
	9		At BAIZIEUX. A/C.R.E. took over duties of Administrative Officer 48th Division (Forward Area) A/Adjutant - Routine.	
	10		At BAIZIEUX. A/C.R.E. - Routine. A/Adjutant - "	
	11		ditto.	
	12		ditto.	

1577 Wt.W10791/1773 500,000 1/15 D. D. & L. A.D.S.S./Forms/C. 2118.

Army Form C. 2118.

WAR DIARY
or
INTELLIGENCE SUMMARY.
(Erase heading not required.)

Instructions regarding War Diaries and Intelligence Summaries are contained in F.S. Regs., Part II. and the Staff Manual respectively. Title pages will be prepared in manuscript.

Place	Date 1917	Hour	Summary of Events and Information	Remarks and references to Appendices
BAIZIEUX.	Jan. 13		At BAIZIEUX. A/C.R.E. - Routine. A/Adjutant - "	
	14		At BAIZIEUX. A/C.R.E. handed over duties of Administrative Officer Forward Area to Staff Captain, 48th Div. Arty. A/Adjutant - Routine. 1/1st S.M. Field Coy. R.E. moved to:- H.Q. and 3 sections at PONT REMY, 1 section at FLIXECOURT.	
	15		At BAIZIEUX. A/C.R.E. - Routine. A/Adjutant - "	
	16		ditto. C.R.E. returned from IIIrd Corps and proceeded for 10 days leave. Adjutant returned from leave and assumed duties of A/C.R.E. from O.C. 1/1st S.M. Field Coy. R.E.	
	17		At BAIZIEUX. A/C.R.E. - Routine. A/Adjutant - "	
	18		At BAIZIEUX. A/C.R.E. visited new area to be taken over from the French for the purpose of valuation of camps. A/Adjutant - Routine.	
	19		At BAIZIEUX. A/C.R.E. visited new area, for valuation. A/Adjutant - Routine.	
	20		At BAIZIEUX. A/C.R.E. visited new area for valuation. A/Adjutant - Routine.	
	21		At BAIZIEUX. ditto. ditto. A/Adjutant - Routine.	

Army Form C. 2118.

WAR DIARY
or
INTELLIGENCE SUMMARY.
(Erase heading not required.)

Instructions regarding War Diaries and Intelligence Summaries are contained in F.S. Regs., Part II. and the Staff Manual respectively. Title pages will be prepared in manuscript.

Place	Date 1917.	Hour	Summary of Events and Information	Remarks and references to Appendices
BAIZIEUX.	Jan. 22		At BAIZIEUX. A/C.R.E. visited new area for valuation. A/Adjutant - Routine.	
	23		At BAIZIEUX. A/C.R.E. visited new area for valuation. A/Adjutant - Routine.	
	24		At BAIZIEUX. A/C.R.E. visited new area for valuation. A/Adjutant - Routine.	
	25		At BAIZIEUX. A/C.R.E. visited new area for valuation. A/Adjutant - Routine.	
CAPPY.	26		~~CAPPY~~ Headquarters R.E. moved to CAPPY. (New area taken over from French) A/C.R.E. - Routine. A/Adjutant - "	
	27		At CAPPY. A/C.R.E. visited new area for valuation. A/Adjutant visited French R.E. Dumps.	
	28		At CAPPY. A/C.R.E. reconnoitred new area for billets. A/Adjutant " " " "	
	29		At CAPPY. C.R.E. returned from leave. Adjutant left for Villers BRETONNEUX for the purpose of valuation of billets in district.	
	30		C.R.E. reconnoitred new area with French Divisional Commander. Adjutant at Villers BRETONNEUX.	

1577 Wt.W10791/1773 500,000 1/15 D.D.&L. A.D.S.S./Forms/C. 2118.

Army Form C. 2118.

WAR DIARY
or
INTELLIGENCE SUMMARY.
(Erase heading not required.)

Place	Date 1917.	Hour	Summary of Events and Information	Remarks and references to Appendices
CAPPY.	Jan. 31st		C.R.E. reconnoitred new front line. Adjutant visited dumps taken over from the French Engineers.	

[signature]
Major R.E.
for C.R.E. 48th Div

Vol 23

CONFIDENTIAL.
****

WAR DIARY,

of

48th (South Midland) Divisional Engineers.

From 1st February 1917...........to...........28th February 1917.

(Volume 24)

Army Form C. 2118.

WAR DIARY
or
INTELLIGENCE SUMMARY.
(Erase heading not required.)

Instructions regarding War Diaries and Intelligence Summaries are contained in F. S. Regs., Part II. and the Staff Manual respectively. Title pages will be prepared in manuscript.

Place	Date 1917	Hour	Summary of Events and Information	Remarks and references to Appendices
CAPPY.	FEB. 1		C.R.E. visited new front line. Adjutant at VILLERS BRETTONEUX taking over property from French Military Authorities.	
	2.		C.R.E., Routine. Adjutant still at VILLERS BRETTONEUX.	
	3.		C.R.E. visited trenches. Adjutant still at VILLERS BRETTONEUX.	
	4.		C.R.E. visited 4th Glosters, Reserve Line, and Support Line. Adjutant still at VILLERS BRETTONEUX.	
	5.		C.R.E. reconnoitred proposed Corps Line with Chief Engineer. Adjutant still at VILLERS BRETTONEUX.	
	6.		C.R.E. visited 143rd Inf. Bde., R.E. Detachment, IGLAU & STETIN Trenches. Adjutant still at VILLERS BRETTONEUX.	
	7.		C.R.E. Routine. Adjutant proceed to CAGNY for duty with Fourth Army, taking over property from French Military Authorities.	
	8.		C.R.E. visited Battn. Hd. Qrs. of 2 Right Battns. of 144th Inf. Bde. and visited R.E. Detachment. Adjutant still at CAGNY.	
	9.		C.R.E. visited Intermediate Line with G.S.O.1. Adjutant still at CAGNY.	
	10.		C.R.E. Routine. Adjutant still at CAGNY.	
	11.		C.R.E. visited Left Sector, and Intermediate Line with G.S.O.1. Adjutant still at CAGNY.	

Army Form C. 2118.

WAR DIARY
or
INTELLIGENCE SUMMARY.

(*Erase heading not required.*)

Instructions regarding War Diaries and Intelligence Summaries are contained in F. S. Regs., Part II and the Staff Manual respectively. Title pages will be prepared in manuscript.

Place	Date 1917.	Hour	Summary of Events and Information	Remarks and references to Appendices
CAPPY.	FEB. 12		C.R.E. visited Front Line, Left Sector, and Right Brigade. Also visited 145th Inf. Bde., R.E. & Pioneer Detachments. Adjutant still at CAGNY.	
	13		C.R.E., Routine. Adjutant still at CAGNY.	
	14		C.R.E. visited Intermediate Line and Divisional Observation Post. Adjutant still at CAGNY.	
	15		C.R.E. Routine. Adjutant still at CAGNY.	
	16		C.R.E. visited Artillery Observation Posts in Left Sector. Adjutant still at CAGNY.	
	17		C.R.E. visited Front Line Right Sector. Also 144th & 145th Brigade Hd. Qrs. Adjutant still at CAGNY.	
	18		C.R.E. Routine. Adjutant still at CAGNY.	
	19		C.R.E. Routine. Adjutant still at CAGNY.	
	20		C.R.E. visited Hd. Qrs. 4/5th, 477th and 5th R.Sussex Pioneers. Adjutant still at CAGNY.	
	21		C.R.E. Routine. Adjutant still at CAGNY.	
	22		C.R.E. Routine. Adjutant still at CAGNY.	

Army Form C. 2118.

WAR DIARY
or
INTELLIGENCE SUMMARY.
(Erase heading not required.)

Instructions regarding War Diaries and Intelligence Summaries are contained in F. S. Regs., Part II. and the Staff Manual respectively. Title pages will be prepared in manuscript.

Place	Date 1917.	Hour	Summary of Events and Information	Remarks and references to Appendices
CAPPY.	FEB. 23		C.R.E. visited HERBECOURT, FLAUCOURT, FEUILLERES Roads and FRISE. Adjutant still at CAGNY.	
	24		C.R.E. went with C.E. to observe line and inspected Communications. Adjutant returned to duty.	
	25		C.R.E. made reconnaissance of River Somme towards BIACHES. Adjutant ditto.	
	26		C.R.E. appointed Chief Engineer 15th Corps and promoted Brigadier-General. Adjutant Routine.	
	27		Adjutant assumed duties of A/C.R.E. and attended Conference at 1st Division Hd. Qrs.	
	28		A/C.R.E. visited Hd. Qrs. of 475th, 477th Field Coys., 5th Sussex Pioneers and 14th Brigade.	

Major R.E.
A/C.R.E. 48th Div

C O N F I D E N T I A L

W A R   D I A R Y

of

48th (South Midland) Divisional Engineers.

From 1st March 1917..........to..........31st March 1917.

(Volume 25)

Army Form C. 2118.

WAR DIARY
or
INTELLIGENCE SUMMARY.

(Erase heading not required.)

Instructions regarding War Diaries and Intelligence Summaries are contained in F. S. Regs., Part II. and the Staff Manual respectively. Title pages will be prepared in manuscript.

Place	Date 1917	Hour	Summary of Events and Information	Remarks and references to Appendices
CAPPY.	May 1st.		A/C.R.E. visited left sector, R.E. Field Coys' Hd. Qrs., Advanced Hd. Qrs. and Brigade Hd. Qrs. A/Adjutant - Routine.	
	2		A/C.R.E., visited left sector. A/Adjutant - Routine.	
	3		Lt.-Col. V.Giles, D.S.O., arrived and assumed the duties of C.R.E. 48th Division. Adjutant - Routine.	
	4		C.R.E. visited front line. Adjutant ditto.	
	5		C.R.E. visited Field Coys' Hd. Qrs. Adjutant attended conference at Fourth Army Hd. Qrs. re taking over and valuation of material and huts from French Army.	
	6		C.R.E., visited IIIrd Corps Hd. Qrs. Adjutant - Routine.	
	7		C.R.E. visited right sector. Adjutant - routine.	
	8		C.R.E. - Routine. Adjutant - do.	
	9		C.R.E. visited 5th R.Sussex Hd. Qrs. Adjutant - Routine	
	10th		C.R.E. visited Corps Line. Adjutant ditto.	
	11th		C.R.E. ditto. Adjutant ditto.	
	12		C.R.E. visited Front Line Adjutant ditto.	

Army Form C. 2118.

WAR DIARY
or
INTELLIGENCE SUMMARY.
(Erase heading not required.)

Instructions regarding War Diaries and Intelligence Summaries are contained in F. S. Regs., Part II. and the Staff Manual respectively. Title pages will be prepared in manuscript.

Place	Date 1917	Hour	Summary of Events and Information	Remarks and references to Appendices
CAPPY.	Mar 13		C.R.E. visited Corps and Army R.E. Dumps. Adjutant ditto.	
	14		C.R.E. visited road construction. Adjutant ditto.	
	15		C.R.E. visited front line. Adjutant ditto.	
	16		C.R.E. visited Front line and site for bridge. Adjutant ditto.	
	17		C.R.E. - Routine. Adjutant attended presentation of med decorations at Div'l Hd. Qrs. by Corps Commander.	
	18		The enemy having retired E. of the SOMME preparations were begun for bridging the river and arrangements made for repair of roads.	
	19		Bridging operations commenced and repair of bridges proceeded with by Field Coys.	
	20		Bridging and repairs to roads proceeded with.	
	21		BIACHES - LA CHAPELLETTE Road opened for traffic 1 Bridge over COLOGNE River completed to take 3 ton lorries. 1 " " " at J.33.c.25 (map 62c -1/40,000) completed by advanced Mobile section. Repairing of roads and filling of craters continued.	
	22		Footbridge at I.33.a.62 (map 62c 1/40,000) completed Second bridge at DOINGT completed to take motor lorries. Bridge at ETERPIGNY completed to take Infantry in fours and light transport.	
	23		3 bridges at PERONNE completed for motor traffic. Road repairs and filling of craters continued.	
	24		LAMIRE Bridge opened for Infantry traffic. TINCOURT Bridge repaired.	

Army Form C. 2118.

WAR DIARY
or
INTELLIGENCE SUMMARY

(Erase heading not required.)

Instructions regarding War Diaries and Intelligence Summaries are contained in F. S. Regs., Part II. and the Staff Manual respectively. Title pages will be prepared in manuscript.

Place	Date 1917	Hour	Summary of Events and Information	Remarks and references to Appendices
PERONNE.	Mar. 25th		Hd. Qrs. R.E. moved to PERONNE. Bridging continued and repair of roads proceeded with.	
	26th		Bridging continued and repair of roads.	
	27th		Bridging and repair of roads continued.	
	28th		ditto. ditto.	
	29th		ditto. ditto.	
	30th		Wooden Girder Bridge over SOMME at PERONNE completed and tested with a fully loaded lorry. Bridge safe for 12 tons. Bridge at BUIRE completed to take G.S. wagons and Field Guns Repair of roads and filling of craters proceeded with.	
	31st		Bridge at DOINGT strengthened to take heavy traffic. Repairs to roads proceeded with.	

Major R.E.
for C.R.E. 48th Div

Vol 25

CONFIDENTIAL
****

WAR DIARY

of

48th (South Midland) Divisional Engineers.

From 1st April 1917..........to............30th April 1917.

(Volume 25)

Army Form C. 2118.

Map - France - 62c.

Instructions regarding War Diaries and Intelligence Summaries are contained in F. S. Regs, Part II. and the Staff Manual respectively. Title pages will be prepared in manuscript.

WAR DIARY
or
INTELLIGENCE SUMMARY.
(Erase heading not required.)

Place	Date 1917	Hour	Summary of Events and Information	Remarks and references to Appendices
PERONNE	April 1		R.E. Hd. Qrs. moved to TINCOURT. PERONNE CANAL, DOINGT, & BUIRE Bridges worked on and improved. The following roads were worked on and kept in a state of repair:- Route from LA CHAPELLETTE through PERONNE. DOINGT - COURCELLES - BUIRE to TINCOURT. TINCOURT - TEMPLEUX LA FOSSE - AIZECOURT. HAMEL - MAISON ROUGE - PERONNE. BUSSU - LONGAVESNES. Wells at VILLERS FAUCON, LONGAVESNES, and TEMPLEUX LA FOSSE, cleared of debris, repaired, & winding gear erected.	
TINCOURT	2		Bridges at PERONNE & DOINGT worked on and kept in a state of repair. Well at EPEHY - F.1.d.08 - put in working order. Dugouts at E.22.a 3 entrances cleared and frames erected.	
	3		Well at DRIENCOURT repaired. Work on railway for Divisional Dump LA CHAPELLETTE commenced. Mine found in cellars and walls of house in VILLERS FAUCON - E.22.d.91. Charges were removed.	
	4		General work on Bridges, Roads, Wells and Dugouts continued.	
	5		ditto. ditto. ditto.	
	6		ditto. ditto. ditto. Siding for Divisional R.E. Dump at LA CHAPELLETTE - formation complete.	
	7		Maintenance of Roads and Bridges procced with. Belt water raiser fixed at well VILLERS FAUCON - E.22.d.76 and troughs for horse watering erected.	
	8		Maintenance of Roads, Bridges, and wells proceeded with.	
	9		Baths at TINCOURT completed.	
	10		General work on Roads, Bridges, Wells etc.	

Army Form C. 2118.

WAR DIARY
or
INTELLIGENCE SUMMARY.
(Erase heading not required.)

Instructions regarding War Diaries and Intelligence Summaries are contained in F. S. Regs. Part II. and the Staff Manual respectively. Title pages will be prepared in manuscript.

Place	Date 1917	Hour	Summary of Events and Information	Remarks and references to Appendices
TINCOURT	April 11		General work on Roads, Wells, Dugouts, etc. continued.	
	12		ditto. ditto. ditto.	
	13		Good supply of water secured from well at VILLERS FAUCON (E.22.d.76) 800 gallons per hour, some doubt about quality of water. Officer's baths at TINCOURT, work proceeding. Improvement of billets at VILLERS FAUCON and LONGAVESNES.	
	14		Well at The Sucrerie ST. EMILIE cleared and chamber at bottom found to have a capacity of 62,000 gals. General work on Roads, Wells, Horse watering arrangements, Billets and wiring of Divisional Front proceeded with.	
	15		General work on Roads, Wells, Horse watering arrangements, Baths, Billets, & Dugouts, proceeded with.	
	16		Well ditto. ditto. ditto. Well at RONSSOY Raperie (F.21.c.16) cleared to depth of 230'. Depth of water 40 feet.	
	17		General work on Roads, Wells, Dugouts, and Billets continued.	
	18		ditto. ditto. Baths at TEMPLEUX completed. Wiring and making Strong Points on Divisional front proceeded with.	
	19		Water raiser and tank for filling water carts and troughs erected at LONGAVESNES (E.25.d.58. Erection of New Divisional Hd. Qrs. at K.11a commenced. Dugouts and Divisional Defences worked on.	
	20		General work on Roads, Wells, Billets and defences for Divisional front proceeded with.	
	21		ditto. ditto. ditto.	
	22		Hd. Qrs. R.E. moved to New Divisional Hd. Qrs. at K.11.a.79	
K.11.a.79	23		General work on Defences, Roads, Wells, Baths, Billets continued.	

Army Form C. 2118.

WAR DIARY
or
INTELLIGENCE SUMMARY.
(Erase heading not required.)

Instructions regarding War Diaries and Intelligence Summaries are contained in F. S. Regs., Part II. and the Staff Manual respectively. Title pages will be prepared in manuscript.

Place	Date 1917	Hour	Summary of Events and Information	Remarks and references to Appendices
K.11.a.79	April 24.		General work on Roads, Wells, Baths, Billets and Defences continued.	
	25		Roads maintained. 6 wells at VILLERS FAUCON cleared of debris. Defences of Division proceeded with.	
	26		Work on Roads, Wells continued. Baths at VILLERS FAUCON opened and 500 men bathed.	
	27		Mine under road at TEMPLEUX LA FOSSE, D.28.d., unloaded. 150 kilos of PERDITE removed and destroyed. General work on Roads, Wells, Baths, Billets and Defences continued.	
	28		Well at ST. EMILIE, The Sucrerie, engine fitted to bed, pumped worked by hand and found to work satisfactorily. General work on Roads, Wells, Baths, Billets and Defences continued.	
	29		General work on Roads, Wells, Baths, Billets, and defences continued.	

Major R.E.
for C.R.E., 48th Division.

Vol 26

CONFIDENTIAL
****

W A R   D I A R Y

o f

48th (South Midland) Divisional Engineers.

From 1st. May 1917......to.....31st May 1917.

(Volume 26)

Army Form C. 2118.

Map - France - 62c. scale 1/40,000.

Instructions regarding War Diaries and Intelligence Summaries are contained in F. S. Regs., Part II. and the Staff Manual respectively. Title pages will be prepared in manuscript.

WAR DIARY
or
INTELLIGENCE SUMMARY
(Erase heading not required.)

Place	Date 1917	Hour	Summary of Events and Information	Remarks and references to Appendices
K.11.a.79	MAY 1		General work on Roads, Wells, Baths, Billets and defences carried out.	
	2		ditto. ditto.	
	3		Hd. Qrs. R.E. moved to PERONNE, on relief by C.R.E. 42nd Division. Work on Corps Roads and maintenance of bridges in and around PERONNE taken over, from 42nd Div'n. Hd. Qrs. of 475th (S.M.) Field Coy. R.E. moved to PERONNE for work on Corps roads and maintenance of bridges. 474th and 477th (S.M.) Field Cos. R.E. remained at EPEHY and VILLERS FAUCON respectively for attachment to C.R.E. 42nd Division for work.	
	4-7		General work on Corps roads, repair of billets, and maintenance of bridges proceeded with.	
	8		C.R.E. reconnoitred new area proposed to be taken over in XVth Corps. Adjutant attended a General Court Martial.	
	9-11		General work on Corps roads, repair of billets, and maintenance of bridges proceeded with.	
	12		C.R.E. reconnoitred new are are to be taken over from C.R.E. 11th Division. 474th (S.M.) Field Coy. R.E. moved to PERONNE and re-joined the Command of the C.R.E. 48th Division. 477th (S.M.) Field Coy. R.E. ditto. ditto.	
	13		General work on Corps roads, repair of billets, and maintenance of bridges proceeded with.	
	14		" " "	
Map - France - 57c	15		- scale 1/40,000 Hd. Qrs. moved to BEAULENCOURT (N.11.central) for relief of 11th Div'l R.E.	
BEAULENCOURT	16		General work on defences and dugouts proceeded with	
	17		Work commenced on BEAUMETZ - MORCHIES line of defence. Dugouts in Left Brigade Sector worked on. Right Brigade Sector- completion of dam in Canal and work on wells proceeded with. General reconnaissance of defences.	
	18		Ditto. ditto. ditto.& Site marked out for new Divisional Hd. Qrs.	

Army Form C. 2118.

WAR DIARY
or
INTELLIGENCE SUMMARY.
(Erase heading not required.)

Instructions regarding War Diaries and Intelligence Summaries are contained in F.S. Regs., Part II. and the Staff Manual respectively. Title pages will be prepared in manuscript.

Place	Date	Hour	Summary of Events and Information	Remarks and references to Appendices
BEAULEN-COURT.	MAY 1917 19/23		Work on BEAUMETZ - MORCHIES defence line continued. " " Dugouts, well at LOUVERVAL and work on defence of Left Sector continued. " " Canal Dam, wells at HERMIES, baths, defence of Right Sector continued. " " erection of new Divisional Hd. Qrs. continued.	
	24		Hd. Qrs. R.E. moved to new Div'l Hd. Qrs. at HAPLINCOURT (I.34.a.25)	
HAPLINCOURT	25/27		Work on BEAUMETZ - MORCHIES defence line continued. " " Dugouts, wells at LOUVERVAL and work on defence of Left Sector continued. " " Canal Dam, wells at HERMIES, baths, defence of Right Sector continued. " " erection of new Divisional Hd. Qrs. continued.	
	28		Canal dam completed. General work on repair of wells, billets, and defences continued.	
	29/31		Work on defences, dugouts, wells, erection of baths, and repair of billets continued.	

Lt.-Col., R.E.
C.R.E., 48th Division.

Vol 27

CONFIDENTIAL
****

W A R   D I A R Y

of

48th (South Midland) Divisional Engineers.

From 1st June 1917....to....30th June 1917.

(Volume 27)

Map - FRANCE - 57c - scale 1/40,000.

Army Form C. 2118.

WAR DIARY
or
INTELLIGENCE SUMMARY

(Erase heading not required.)

Instructions regarding War Diaries and Intelligence Summaries are contained in F. S. Regs, Part II. and the Staff Manual respectively. Title pages will be prepared in manuscript.

Place	Date	Hour	Summary of Events and Information	Remarks and references to Appendices
HAPLINCOURT. (I 34 a 25)	1917. June. 1		Major G.F.Eberle, O.C. 475th Fd. Co. R.E. arrived at C.R.E's Hd. Qrs. for one month's course as C.R.E. General work of Wiring, construction of dugouts, and repair of roads proceeded with.	
	2/3		Sinking of wells, construction of dugouts, and wiring of defence lines proceeded with.	
	4		do. do. do. do. Major E.Briggs, O.C. 477th Fd. Co. R.E. awarded D.S.O. in Birthday Honours List.	
	5/7		Work of screening roads, construction of dugouts and O.P's., also wiring of defence lines proceeded with.	
	8		During night 7/8 a raid was made by 1st Bucks Battn. on an enemy post. A party of R.E. under 2/Lt. Maclennan, A.G., of 477th Fd. Co. R.E. went forward for consolidation purposes with successful results and for which 2/Lt. A.G.Maclennan was awarded the Military Cross.	
	9		Work continued on Haymaking, screening of roads, construction of dugouts and wiring of Defence Lines.	
	10/14		do. do. on do. do. do. do. Making up of trestles for future bridging operations commenced.	
	15/19		Repair of BEAUMETZ - HERMIES Road proceeded with and a footbridge across Canal du Nord completed. General work on defences continued.	
	20/28		Screening of roads, construction of dugouts, and wiring of defence lines continued. Petrol Pump (6000) gallons per hour) placed in position in chamber of well in LOUVERVAL. Chain Helice well at DOIGNIES (J.16.a.55) dismantled and re-erected with windlass. Good well in DEMICOURT cleaned out and fitted with Belt Water Raiser.	
	29/31		General work on screening of roads, repair of roads, construction of dugouts and O.Ps., and wiring of Defence lines proceeded with.	

CONFIDENTIAL
****

WAR   DIARY

of

48th (South Midland) Divisional Engineers.

From 1st July 1917....to....31st July 1917.

(Volume 28)

Army Form C. 2118.

WAR DIARY
INTELLIGENCE SUMMARY.

Map. FRANCE - 57C - Scale 1/40,000

Place	Date 1917	Hour	Summary of Events and Information	Remarks and references to Appendices
WAPLINCOURT (I.34.a.25)	July 1/3		Handing over work to E.R.E. 3rd Division	
	4		Moved to GOMIECOURT	
GOMIECOURT	5		Proceeded to ACHIET LE GRAND to entrain for HOPOUTRE siding R. POPERINGHE Belgium. Left ACHIET LE GRAND at 4 p.m.	
Map - BELGIUM - 28 - scale 1/40,000.				
	6		Arrived at HOPOUTRE at 5 a.m. Breakfasted and proceeded to Camp situated 2000 yds N. of BRANDHOEK R.24.d.4.2. Arrived 10 a.m. and settled down for 5 days rest & training.	
	7		Considerable shelling of camp took place in the afternoon causing several casualties in the 3 Field Coys amongst men & horses. The 3 Field Coys moved at night to other sites & Hd. Qrs. R.E. moved to Divisional Camp recently evacuated by 39 Divn at A.30.c.57.	
	8		The 3 Field Coys moved to L Camp R. WATOU, L.30.53, (sheet 27) for remainder of resting period. Hd. Qrs. R.E. remained at A.30 & 57.	
	11		The 3 Field Coys came under orders of C.R.E. 39 Division attached.	
	12		Hd. Qrs. of 3 Field Coys moved to Camp at A.21.a.87.	
	13		At 6-30 a.m. to 7 a.m. considerable shelling of Divisional Camp in which Hd. Qrs. R.E. was situated & caused the wounding of T/Lieut E.A. Sainsbury Adjutant 48th Div R.E. Owing to persistent shelling Hd. Qrs. R.E. moved to transport lines at PESEL HOEK A.21.a.84.	

Army Form C. 2118.

WAR DIARY
or
INTELLIGENCE SUMMARY.
(Erase heading not required.)

Instructions regarding War Diaries and Intelligence Summaries are contained in F.S. Regs., Part II. and the Staff Manual respectively. Title pages will be prepared in manuscript.

Place	Date 1917	Hour	Summary of Events and Information	Remarks and references to Appendices
	July 14/23		3 Field Companies engaged on work under C.R.E. 39th Div.	
	24		Hd. Qrs. 48th Div. arrived at Divisional Camp lately occupied by 39th Div. Hd. Qrs. R.E. moved & joined 48th Division at this Camp.	
	25		All section of 3 Field Coys working in forward area under C.R.E. 39 Div returned to Camp at PESELHOEK Q21A57 and came under orders of C.E. 18th Corps.	
	26/29		All 3 Field Coys reinforced & rested preparing to proceeding to forward area for work under C.E. 18th Corps in conjunction with impending attack from 5th Army Front.	
	30"		Three Field Coys moved to forward billets at Hzc for work on roads & tracks under C.E. 18th Corps.	
	31"		General work on roads & tracks.	

VR Hule
Capt. R.E.
for C.R.E. 48th Div

Vol 29

CONFIDENTIAL
****
W A R   D I A R Y

o f

48th (South Midland) Divisional Engineers.

From 1st August 1917 to 31st August 1917.

(Volume 29)

Army Form C. 2118.

Map BELGIUM - 28 - scale 1/40,000

WAR DIARY
or
INTELLIGENCE SUMMARY.
(Erase heading not required.)

Instructions regarding War Diaries and Intelligence Summaries are contained in F. S. Regs., Part II. and the Staff Manual respectively. Title pages will be prepared in manuscript.

Place	Date 1917	Hour	Summary of Events and Information	Remarks and references to Appendices
Border Camp. Nr. POPERINGHE.	Aug. 1/4		Three Field Coys. employed on making of Roads, tracks, and overland Trenchboard Tracks in the Forward area.	
	5		Three Field Coys. moved to Billets of Field Coys. of 39th Division.	
	6		Headquarters of 48th Div. R.E. moved to "C" Camp (G.6.b.19) Nr. POPERINGHE.	
	7/8		Three Field Coys. employed on making of roads, tracks, dugouts and improving accommodation.	
	9/15		do. do. do.	
			Pack Horse transport used nightly for conveying of R.E. material up to forward R.E. Dumps preparatory to an attack on 16th inst August	
	16		C.R.E. and Adjutant moved to advanced Headquarters at Canal Bank at C.25.d.14. 2 sections R.E. and 2 Platoons were employed on consolidation of ground won during the day in the vicinity of JEWS HILL, HILLOCK FARM, and BORDER HOUSE. Strong posts made at MISC du M Bou	
	17/19		General work on maintenance of roads, tracks, and improving accommodation in the forward area by the three Field Coys.	
	19		1 section R.E. consolidated ground won by 8th Worcs. 1 section R.E. consolidated HILLOCK FARM (C.12.a.65)	
	20/21		General work on maintenance and making of roads, tracks, and improving accommodation in the forward area.	
	21		Road bridge ST.JULIEN over STEENBEEK repaired and made passable for tanks.	
	22/24		General work proceeded with.	
	25		Assembly trenches covered with camouflage to conceal the Infantry who intended making a daylight attack. This proved most successful.	
	26		Work continued on accommodation, roads, tracks, etc.	

Army Form C. 2118.

WAR DIARY
or
INTELLIGENCE SUMMARY.
(Erase heading not required.)

Instructions regarding War Diaries and Intelligence Summaries are contained in F. S. Regs., Part II. and the Staff Manual respectively. Title pages will be prepared in manuscript.

Place	Date 1917	Hour	Summary of Events and Information	Remarks and references to Appendices
CANAL BANK Nr. YPRES.	Aug. 27		Attack by 144th Inf. Bde. 1 section standing by for consolidation work.	
	28		Work continued on accommodation, trenchboard tracks, roads, etc. in the forward area.	
	29		48th Divisional R.E. relieved by 58th Divisional R.E. and companies moved to billets in back area. C.R.E. Headquarters moved to billets at Div'l R.E. Store on POPERINGHE-ELVERDINGHE Road.	
	30/31	1430	1 Company employed on roads in the forward area. 2 Companies employed on (Hutting and) improving billets in back area.	

Capt. & Adjt. R.E.
for C.R.E., 48th Division.

Vol 30

CONFIDENTIAL
****

WAR DIARY

of

48th (South Midland) Divisional Engineers.

From 1st September 1917 to 30th September 1917.

(Volume 30)

Army Form C. 2118.

WAR DIARY

Map - BELGIUM - Sheet 28 - scale 1/40,000

Instructions regarding War Diaries and Intelligence Summaries are contained in F.S. Regs., Part II. and the Staff Manual respectively. Title pages will be prepared in manuscript.

(Erase heading not required.)

Place	Date 1917	Hour	Summary of Events and Information	Remarks and references to Appendices
POPERINGHE-ELVERDINGHE ROAD, A.23.c.14	Sep. 1-8		Three Field Coys. employed on forward roads, camps and repair of dugouts in the forward area, and training.	
	9		Companies employed as above. Adjutant proceeded to England on 10 days leave.	
	10/14		General work on roads, camps and repair of dugouts and billets in forward area, and Canal Bank.	
	15		H.Q. and Nos. 1 & 4 sections of 477th Field Coys. moved to PROVEN for work under C.R.E., Fifth Army Troops. Nos. 2 & 3 sections of 477th Fd. Co. R.E. moved to ST. JANSTER BIEZEN and were attached to 144th Inf. Bde. and moved with them to LA RECOUSEE Area (Back) for R.E. Services.	
	16/26		General work on forward roads, camps, dugouts, etc. proceeded with.	
	27		Nos. 474 and 475 Field Coys. moved to billets on Canal Bank and took over work from Field Coys. of 58th Division.	
	28		Headquarters of C.R.E., 48th Division moved to BRAKE CAMP, G.6.b.19, on Division returning from Back Training Area. Major H.Clissold,D.S.O.,Officer Commanding 474th Field Coy. R.E. was killed by enemy artillery whilst inspecting work on dugouts in forward area. Hd. Qrs. and Nos. 1 & 4 sections of 477th Field Coy. R.E. moved from PROVEN to camp at PESELHOEK, A.21.a.87 and came under orders of C.R.E., 48th Division.	
BRAKE CAMP.	29		474 and 475 Field Coys. proceeded with work as taken over from Field Coys. of 58th Division which included laying of tramlines, trenchboard tracks and work on shelters in CALIFORNIA Trench.	
	30		Hd. Qrs. and Nos. 1 & 4 sections of 477th Fd. Coys. moved to billets on CANAL BANK preparatory to commencing work as taken over from Field Coy. of 58th Division.	

CONFIDENTIAL
****

W A R   D I A R Y

O F

48th (South Midland) Divisional Engineers.

From 1st October 1917 to 31st October 1917.

(Volume 31)

Army Form C. 2118.

WAR DIARY
of
INTELLIGENCE SUMMARY.
(Erase heading not required.)

"haf" - BELGIUM - Sheet 28.- scale 1/40,000

Instructions regarding War Diaries and Intelligence Summaries are contained in F. S. Regs., Part II. and the Staff Manual respectively. Title pages will be prepared in manuscript.

Place	Date	Hour	Summary of Events and Information	Remarks and references to Appendices
BRAKE CAMP G.6.C.10	1917 Oct. 1/2		3 Field Coy engaged on erecting shelters in old German front line, repairing dugouts, repair of pillbox road, laying Decauville tramline & trenchboard track to front line.	
	3		C.R.E. Hd. Qrs. moved to billets in Canal Bank C.25.d.15	
	4/9		The Division on these dates was involved in operations which resulted in several advances of its front. The 3 Field Coy was employed, together with the assistance of 249 Field Coy R.E. and large working parties from the Royal Naval Division (63rd), on improving forward communication by making temporary roads, laying trenchboard tracks & tramline what greatly facilitated operations & owing to its inclement weather anyone not uninvited was unpossible without these. Assistance was also given to the Artillery by making & laying portable tracks which consisted of rolls of Wire netting & rolls wooden slats for use across at intervals of about 2'-6". By the use of these tracks the Artillery were enabled to man-handle their guns to new forward positions, necessitated by the Infantry advancing & leaping objectives, over ground which was too muddy for horse haulage. These tracks were proved of various objectives to be captured and proved of great help in guiding Infantry ration parties & other working parties across them to newly captured territory.	

Army Form C. 2118.

WAR DIARY
or
INTELLIGENCE SUMMARY.
(Erase heading not required.)

Instructions regarding War Diaries and Intelligence Summaries are contained in F.S. Regs. Part II. and the Staff Manual respectively. Title pages will be prepared in manuscript.

Place	Date 1916	Hour	Summary of Events and Information	Remarks and references to Appendices
Canal Bank C.25.d.15.	Oct.		Map – BELGIUM – sheet 28 – scale 1/40,000	
	9/9		A portion of the 48th Divis. R.E. were also employed on providing a considerable amount of forward accommodation & water points to enable troops to be accommodated as near as possible to the front line.	
	10"		474 Fd. Coy. moved back to BROWNE CAMP A.22.d.55. 475 & 477 Fd. Coy. do. do. do.	Relieved by R.E. of 9th Divn.
	11"		CRE's H.Q. moved back to Divisional Workshop on POPERINGHE-ELVERDINGHE Road, A.23.c.14, on being relieved by CRE 9th Divn.	
	12"		48th Divisional R.E. rested & made preparation for entraining at PESELHOEK	
	13"		CRE's H.Q's & 474 Fd. Coy entrained at PESELHOEK for new area. 475 Fd. Coy do.	
	14"		CRE's H.Q's arrived at MAROEUIL, near ARRAS, detrained and marched to billets at LA TARGETTE, F.12.d.65, Map – FRANCE – 51c – 1/40,000.	
LA TARGETTE	15/16		Map – France – 51c – 1/40,000	
			475 & 477 Fd. Coy. arrived at MAROEUIL & detrained	
	16"		B.2 Fd. Coy accommodated at LA TARGETTE (A.2.c + A.1.d)	
			1 Fd. Coy do. do. Aux REITZ (A.8.c.)	
	17/18		Work taken over from # 2nd Canadian Divisional R.E.	

WAR DIARY
or
INTELLIGENCE SUMMARY.
(Erase heading not required.)

Army Form C. 2118.

Place	Date	Hour	Summary of Events and Information	Remarks and references to Appendices
LA TARGETTE	1917 Oct 19/31		Map – France – 51c – 1/40,000 48th Divisional R.E. were engaged on provision of Winter accommodation which included repair of huts, transport lines, horse standings, & baths in near Divisional area. Also making of dugout, erection of shelters, improvements to Left & Right Bde. H.Q., and renewing of communications (including trench tram tracks, overland routes & communication trenches) in the forward Divisional Area.	

J F Hale
Capt. & Adj. R.E.
For C.R.E. 48th. Div.